**W9-DFE-826**

# NOIR MOVIES

## FACTS, FIGURES & FUN

*"Any book without a mistake in it has had too much money spent on it"*

Sir William Collins, publisher

# NOIR MOVIES

## FACTS, FIGURES & FUN

## JOHN GRANT

*ff&f*

For Barbara and Randy Dannenfelser

Noir Movies
Facts, Figures & Fun

Published by
Facts, Figures & Fun, an imprint of
AAPPL Artists' and Photographers' Press Ltd.
10 Hillside, London SW19 4NH, UK
info@ffnf.co.uk   www.ffnf.co.uk
info@aappl.com   www.aappl.com

Sales and Distribution
UK and export: Turnaround Publisher Services Ltd.
orders@turnaround-uk.com
USA and Canada: Sterling Publishing Inc. sales@sterlingpub.com
Australia & New Zealand: Peribo Pty. peribomec@bigpond.com
South Africa: Trinity Books. trinity@iafrica.com

A catalogue record for this book is available from the
British Library.
ISBN 13: 9781904332398
ISBN 10: 1904332390

Design (contents and cover): Malcolm Couch
mal.couch@blueyonder.co.uk

Printed in China by Imago Publishing
info@imago.co.uk

For information about custom editions, special sales, premium
and corporate purchases, please contact ffnf Special Sales
+44 20 8971 2094 or info@ffnf.co.uk

# CONTENTS

So What Do You Mean by *Noir*? 7

Dashiell Hammett and the Movies 10

They Shot at Night with Gun and Camera:
The Great *Noir* Directors 15
*Claude Chabrol – Billy Wilder*

Raymond Chandler and the Movies 39

A Library of Classic-Era *Noir* 43
*1941: Citizen Kane – 1962: The Manchurian Candidate*

James M. Cain and the Movies 52

A Library of Neo-*Noir* 57
*1971: Klute – 2004: Collateral*

Cornell Woolrich and the Movies 66

A Library of International *Noir* 73
*1940: Gaslight – 2002: Dirty Pretty Things*

Jim Thompson and the Movies 81

A Library of Fantasy *Noir* 85
*1942: Cat People – 2004: The Forgotten*

Patricia Highsmith and the Movies 89

The Edgar Awards 93

Bibliography 96

# SO WHAT DO YOU MEAN BY *NOIR?*

The term *film noir* was coined by the French to describe the new breed of cinema they perceived at the end of WWII when suddenly they were able to see several years' worth of American movies that had been barred from them during the Nazi occupation.

The term derived from the name of a highly successful line of American and pseudo-American hardboiled mysteries published by Gallimard under the series title *Série Noire*; the series was so-called because of the books' uniform black covers. The French saw the movies as being the cinematic equivalent of those books.

It was some considerable while before the term was adopted in the movies' homeland, the USA, and certainly the makers of the movies that represent *noir*'s Golden Age never thought of themselves as having created a particular genre; to them these movies were simply crime thrillers that reflected the current popularity of hardboiled novels among the reading public. Most were intended as B-movies, which meant they should be short and cheap.

The demise of the B-movie toward the end of the 1950s brought a sharp and almost terminal drop in the number of *noir* movies being made, and often 1959 or 1960 is fingered as the year in which true *film noir* ended, with the baton being picked up again in the later 1980s by the makers of consciously neo-*noir* movies. But *noir* moviemaking never stopped during the intervening years. Further, foreign moviemakers – notably the French – continued to make *noirs* virtually unabated.

*Film noir* didn't spring from nowhere, of course. These movies – cheap, short, pithy – had their roots in a form of literature that shared exactly those qualities and was, to boot, hugely popular: pulp hardboiled fiction. At about the same time that *film noir* was gearing up, this form of literature was, thanks to writers like Raymond Chandler, just starting to raise its sights above the level of the pulp paperback, and meanwhile the literary powers-that-be recognized that, while much of it was derivative trash, the same could be said of *any* form of fiction: there were jewels among the dross. There would prove a similar lag before cinema scholars realized that among those B-movies they'd been ignoring were many masterpieces.

The visual style of *film noir* came about because of the Nazis' ascendancy in Germany and then conquest of much of Europe. From the mid-1930s onward, many European moviemakers fled to the relative safety of the US. They brought with them a style of moviemaking, realist Expressionism, that Hollywood had largely ignored. The insularity of the US movie industry meant these newcomers could find it hard to get jobs directing the plum movies, and so they often joined the B-movie factories. The result was that, not infrequently, B-movies proved better – and have survived longer – than the A-movies they were made to support.

*Noir* was, therefore, never a conscious genre. What made a movie a *film noir* had something to do with style, something to do with theme, and perhaps most importantly something to do with worldview:

- human beings were always fallible and often corrupt;

- the fates were fickle and could pick upon anyone, anywhere, as their victim;

- the wages of even the slightest sin were likely to be death or at the very least social destruction;

- and the most the good guys could generally hope for was a temporary victory.

Today we have the good fortune to be living through the second Golden Age of *film noir*. The style is hugely popular among moviemakers and general public alike: at the time of writing, at least two US television channels are running *noir*/neo-*noir* seasons that show no signs of ever ending. The same can be said of *noir*'s second Golden Age.

**A Note on Abbreviations**

dir=directed by

scr=screenplay by

vt=variant/alternative title

# DASHIELL HAMMETT
# AND
# THE MOVIES

Samuel Dashiell Hammett was born in Maryland in 1891 and as a young man worked for the Pinkerton Detective Agency. Forced to quit for health reasons, he began writing in 1922, and soon was a regular contributor to the pulp magazine *Black Mask*. Many of his early stories featured the Continental Op, who worked for a detective agency much like Pinkertons. Hammett's first two novels, *Red Harvest* (1929) and *The Dain Curse* (1929), featured the Op; his next, *The Maltese Falcon* (1930), introduced Sam Spade. *The Glass Key* (1931) brought yet another protagonist, Ned Beaumont. With *The Thin Man* (1934) Hammett turned away from the hardboiled genre to produce a society mystery. Among other activities, he wrote scripts for several movies. He served a six-month jail sentence in 1951 for resisting the McCarthy witch-hunts.

Hammett died in 1961 of lung cancer. All his novels were filmed, and *The Thin Man* sparked off a series.

## RED HARVEST

The first movie adaptation of this novel was, incredibly, *Roadhouse Nights* (1930; vt *The River Inn*), dir Hobart Henley, scr Garrett Fort, storied by Ben Hecht, starring Jimmy Durante with his old vaudeville partners Lou Clayton and Eddie Jackson; t'ain't like any Hammett novel you ever read.

Although uncredited, *Red Harvest* served as a basis, along with *The Glass Key*, for the Coen Brothers' *Miller's Crossing* (1990), dir Joel Coen. Akira Kurosawa's *Yojimbo* (1961) was another to draw upon the novel; since Sergio Leone's *A Fistful of Dollars* (1964) was based on *Yojimbo*, one finds Hammett's influence in unexpected places.

## THE MALTESE FALCON

First filmed in 1931 as *The Maltese Falcon* (vt *Dangerous Female*), dir Roy Del Ruth. Ricardo Cortez was an obnoxiously smug Sam Spade, Bebe Daniels better as the temptress Ruth Wonderly. Maude Fulton was principal scripter.

Almost forgotten is the 1935 remake, *Satan Met a Lady*, dir William Dieterle, scr Brown Holmes. Warren William played suave detective Ted Shane (rather than hardboiled Sam Spade) and the quest was for not a falcon but the fabled Horn of Roland. Bette Davis was the *femme fatale*.

The 1941 version, dir and scr John Huston, starred Humphrey Bogart as Spade and Mary Astor as Brigid O'Shaughnessy – not to forget Peter Lorre as Joel Cairo and Sydney Greenstreet as Kasper Gutman – and is one of the great classics of *film noir*. Would this have been so had it been released under its working title, *The Gent from Frisco*? We shall never know . . .

*"Don't worry about the story's goofiness.*
*A sensible one would have had us all in the cooler."*
The Maltese Falcon (1941)

## THE THIN MAN

Hammett's 1934 novel was a lighthearted mystery with a married couple, Nick and Nora Charles, as wisecracking detectives. The 1934 movie *The Thin Man*, dir W.S. Van Dyke, starring William Powell and Myrna Loy, matched the novel well. It gave rise to a series: *After the Thin Man* (1936), *Another Thin Man* (1939; vt *Return of the Thin Man*), *Shadow of the Thin Man* (1941), *The Thin Man Goes Home* (1945) and *Song of the Thin Man* (1947). There was also a TV series, *The Thin Man*, which ran 1957–9 and starred Peter Lawford and Phyllis Kirk as the Charleses.

● Not to be forgotten in the series' cast is the Charleses' yappy little dog, Asta. In one of many recursive references in Robert Altman's 1973 *The Long Goodbye*, Marlowe calls a dog Asta as if this were a generic name for irritating small dogs.

## THE GLASS KEY

First filmed as more of a melodrama than a crime tale. *The Glass Key* (1935) had a cast including George Raft, Claire Dodd, Edward Arnold and Ray Milland. The plot was oversimplified, and Frank Tuttle's direction was pedestrian.

The far superior remake was *The Glass Key* (1942), dir Stuart Heisler, scr Jonathan Latimer. Alan Ladd was Ned Beaumont, Brian Donlevy was Paul Madvig, Veronica Lake was the quasi *femme fatale* Janet Henry, and Joseph Calleia was gangster boss Nick Varna.

A less-known remake is the Russian movie *Svora* (1985; vt *Bande*), a fairly faithful adaptation of the novel, dir Arvo Kruusement, scr Nikolai Ivanov; Tõnu Kark was Beaumont, Aarne Üksküla was Madvig and Mara Zvajgzne was Janet.

## THE DAIN CURSE

Although this hasn't been filmed for the cinema, it was in 1978 adapted as a six-hour TV miniseries. E.W. Swackhamer directed a cast including James Coburn as hardboiled P.I. Hamilton Nash in a case involving a stolen case of diamonds and an ancient family curse.

## OTHERS

In 1934–5 Hammett scripted artist Alex Raymond's newspaper comic strip *Secret Agent X–9*, and a couple of cinema serials were based on this (with Hammett uncredited): both called simply *Secret Agent X–9*, they came in 1937, dir Ford Beebe and Clifford Smith, and 1945, dir Lewis D. Collins and Ray Taylor.

Movies have been made of some of Hammett's short stories, too. The 1924 Continental Op story "The House in Turk Street" has been filmed as *The House on Turk Street* (2002; vt *No Good Deed*), dir Bob Rafelson, with Samuel L. Jackson in the lead. Hammett wrote original stories for the movies *City Streets* (1931), dir Rouben Mamoulian, the Fay Wray screamie *Woman in the Dark* (1934; vt *Women in the Shadows*), dir Phil Rosen, and *Mister Dynamite* (1935), dir Alan Crosland, and adapted a play by his partner Lillian Hellman for the screen as *Watch on the Rhine* (1943), dir Herman Shumlin.

Joe Gores's 1975 novel *Hammett*, featuring Hammett as a character dragged into a mystery involving kidnap and murder, was filmed by Wim Wenders in 1982, scr Dennis O'Flaherty and Ross Thomas; Frederic Forrest starred as Hammett. The production was not untroubled: reaction to Wenders's first cut was such that he was made to reshoot some three-quarters of the movie.

# THEY SHOT AT NIGHT: THE GREAT *NOIR* DIRECTORS

Countless directors have contributed to the development of *film noir* as a distinctive style; many of the earlier ones are now known only to cinema scholars and devotees. Here we look at just a few of *film noir*'s great directing heroes.

##  CLAUDE CHABROL

Born in Paris in 1930, Claude Chabrol is widely regarded as the founder of the movement in French cinema known as the *Nouvelle Vague*; he has been (like Henri-Georges Clouzot before him) called The French Hitchcock, and he makes no secret of his admiration for Hitchcock's works – his first movie, *Le Beau Serge* (1958), was derived from Hitchcock's *Shadow of a Doubt* (1943). Through his long career he has built up an impressive body of psychological thrillers, most of them unabashedly *noir*.

### Select Filmography
1958    *Le Beau Serge*, vt *Bitter Reunion*, vt *Handsome Serge*
1959    *Les Cousins*, vt *The Cousins*
        *À Double Tour*, vt *Leda*, vt *Web of Passion*
1960    *Les Bonnes Femmes*, vt *The Girls*, vt *The Good Girls*,
            vt *The Good Time Girls*
1961    *Les Godelureaux*, vt *Wise Guys*
1962    *L'Oeil du Malin*, vt *The Third Lover*
1963    *Landru*, vt *Bluebeard*
        *Ophélia*

1964   *Le Tigre Aime la Chair Fraiche*, vt *Code Name Tiger*, vt
         *The Tiger Likes Fresh Blood*
1965   *Marie-Chantal Contre le Docteur Kha*, vt *Blue Panther*
         *Le Tigre se Parfume à la Dynamite*, vt *An Orchid for the Tiger*,
           vt *Our Agnt Tiger*
1966   *La Ligne de Démarcation*, vt *Line of Demarcation*
1967   *La Route de Corinthe*, vt *Criminal Story*, vt *The Road to Corinth*,
           vt *Who's Got the Black Box*
         *Le Scandale*, vt *The Champagne Murders*
1968   *Les Biches*, vt *Bad Girls*, vt *Girlfriends*, vt *The Does*
1969   *La Femme Infidèle*, vt *The Unfaithful Wife*
         *Que la Bête Meure*, vt *Killer!*, vt *The Beast Must Die*, vt
           *This Man Must Die*
1970   *Le Boucher*, vt *The Butcher*
         *La Rupture*, vt *The Break Up*
1971   *La Décade Prodigieuse*, vt *Ten Days Wonder*
         *Juste Avant la Nuit*, vt *Just Before Nightfall*
1972   *Docteur Popaul*, vt *Dr Popaul*, vt *High Heels*, vt *Play Now,*
           *Pay Later*, vt *Scoundrel in White*
1973   *Les Noces Rouges*, vt *Wedding in Blood*
1974   *Nada*, vt *The Nada Gang*
1975   *Les Innocents aux Mains Sales*, vt *Dirty Hands*,
           vt *Innocents with Dirty Hands*
         *Une Partie de Plaisir*, vt *A Piece of Pleasure*, vt *Pleasure Party*
1976   *Folies Bourgeoises*, vt *The Twist*
         *Les Magiciens*, vt *Death Rite*
1977   *Alice ou La Dernière Fugue*, vt *Alice*, vt *Alice or The Last Escapade*
1978   *Les Liens de Sang*, vt *Blood Relatives*
         *Violette Nozière*, vt *Violette*
1980   *Le Cheval d'Orgueil*, vt *The Horse of Pride*, vt *The Proud Ones*
1981   *Le Affinités Électives*, vt *Les Affinités*
         *Le Système du Docteur Goudron et du Professeur Plume*
1982   *La Danse de Mort*
         *Les Fantômes du Chapelier*, vt *The Hatter's Ghost*
         *M. le Maudit*
1984   *Le Sang des Autres*, vt *The Blood of Others*
1985   *Poulet au Vinaigre*, vt *Cop au Vin*
1986   *Inspecteur Lavardin*, vt *L'Inspecteur Lavardin ou La Justice*
1987   *Le Cri du Hibou*, vt *The Cry of the Owl*
         *Masques*, vt *Masks*
1988   *Une Affaire des Femmes*, vt *Story of Women*

1990    Dr M, vt Club Extinction
        Jours Tranquilles à Clichy, vt Quiet Days in Clichy
1991    Madame Bovary
1992    Betty
1993    L' Oeil de Vichy, vt The Eye of Vichy
1994    L'Enfer, vt Hell, vt Jealousy, vt Torment
1995    La Cérémonie, vt A Judgement in Stone
1996    Cyprien Katsaris
1997    Rien ne Va Plus, vt The Swindle
1999    Au Coeur du Mensonge, vt At the Heart of the Lie,
                vt The Color of Lies
2000    Merci pour le Chocolat, vt Nightcap
2003    La Fleur du Mal, vt The Flower of Evil
2004    La Demoiselle d'Honneur
2005    La Comédie du Pouvoir

## 🎬 HENRI-GEORGES CLOUZOT 🎬

Born in Niort, France, in 1907, Clouzot was initially involved with
the movies as a screenwriter, a profession he never gave up even
after becoming a successful director. He was also often called The
French Hitchcock, and the British director certainly considered
there was a rivalry between the two – something Hitchcock,
being Hitchcock, did not like one bit. Clouzot would have made
far more movies had it not been for protracted bouts of poor
health. His best-known movie is undoubtedly Les Diaboliques
(1955). He died in Paris in 1977.

### Select Filmography

1931    La Terreur des Batignolles
1933    Caprice de Princesse
        Tout pour l'Amour
1942    L'Assassin Habite . . .
            au 21, vt The Murderer
            Lives at Number 21
1943    Le Corbeau, vt The Raven
1947    Quai des Orfèvres,
            vt Jenny Lamour
1949    Manon
1950    Miquette et sa Mère,
            vt Miquette

1953    Le Salaire de la Peur,
            vt The Wages of Fear
1955    Les Diaboliques,
            vt Diabolique, vt The
            Devils, vt The Fiends
1956    Le Mystère Picasso, vt
            The Mystery of Picasso
1957    Les Espions, vt The Spies
1960    La Vérité, vt The Truth
1964    L'Enfer
1968    La Prisonnière, vt Female
            Prisoner, vt Woman
            in Chains

##  BRIAN DE PALMA

Born in Newark, New Jersey, in 1940, De Palma has through much of his career displayed an overt indebtedness to Alfred Hitchcock, whom he has homaged time and again – he even commissioned scores from Bernard Herrmann, the composer widely known for his Hitchcock scores. De Palma has been much praised – as well as much condemned – for his "voyeuristic" style, which can on occasion seem to verge on the pornographic.

### Select Filmography

1960 *Icarus*

1962 *Woton's Wake*

1964 *Jennifer*

1966 *The Responsive Eye*

1968 *Greetings*

1969 *The Wedding Party*

1970 *Dionysus*, vt *Dionysus in '69*
Hi, Mom!,
   vt *Blue Manhattan*,
   vt *Confessions of a Peeping John*,
   vt *Son of Greetings*

1973 *Sisters*, vt *Blood Sisters*

1974 *Phantom of the Paradise*

1976 *Carrie*
*Obsession*

1978 *The Fury*

1979 *Home Movies*,
   vt *The Maestro*

1980 *Dressed to Kill*

1981 *Blow Out*

1983 *Scarface*

1984 *Body Double*

1986 *Wise Guys*

1987 *The Untouchables*

1989 *Casualties of War*

1990 *The Bonfire of the Vanities*

1992 *Raising Cain*

1993 *Carlito's Way*

1996 *Mission: Impossible*

1998 *Snake Eyes*

2000 *Mission to Mars*

2002 *Femme Fatale*

2005 *Toyer*

2006 *The Black Dahlia*

*"Remarks want you to make them.*
*They got their tongues hanging out waiting to be said."*
Murder, My Sweet (1944)

##  EDWARD DMYTRYK

Born in Grand Forks, British Columbia, Canada in 1908, Dmytryk had a troubled childhood in San Francisco. His first job was as a studio messenger; he rose through the ranks to become a much favoured director. His career was stalled during the McCarthy witch-hunts; he initially refused to cooperate with the House Un-American Activities Committee, served a term in prison, and then recanted, publicly naming names. He spent the latter part of his career as a university professor, lecturing on aspects of the movies. He died in 1999 in Encino, California.

## Select Filmography

1935 *The Hawk,*
        vt *Trail of the Hawk*
1939 *Television Spy*
1940 *Emergency Squad*
    *Golden Gloves*
    *Her First Romance,*
        vt *The Right Man*
    *Mystery Sea Raider*
1941 *Confessions of Boston Blackie*
    *Secrets of the Lone Wolf*
    *Sweetheart of the Campus,*
        vt *Broadway Ahead*
    *The Blonde From Singapore,*
        vt *Hot Pearls*
    *The Devil Commands,*
        vt *The Devil Said No,*
        vt *When the Devil Commands*
    *Under Age*
1942 *Counter-Espionage*
    *Seven Miles from Alcatraz*
1943 *Behind the Rising Sun*
    *Captive Wild Woman*
1943 *Hitler's Children*
    *Tender Comrade*
    *The Falcon Strikes Back*

1944 *Murder, My Sweet,*
        vt *Farewell, My Lovely*
1945 *Back to Bataan,*
        vt *The Invisible Army*
    *Cornered*
1946 *Till the End of Time*
1947 *Crossfire*
    *So Well Remembered*
1949 *Give Us This Day,*
        vt *Christ in Concrete,*
        vt *Salt and the Devil,*
        vt *Salt to the Devil*
    *Obsession,* vt *The Hidden Room*
1952 *Eight Iron Men*
    *Mutiny*
    *The Sniper*
1953 *The Juggler*
    *Three Lives*
1954 *Broken Lance*
    *The Caine Mutiny*
1955 *Soldier of Fortune*
    *The End of the Affair*
    *The Left Hand of God*
1956 *The Mountain*
1957 *Raintree County*
1958 *The Young Lions*
1959 *The Blue Angel*

|  |  |  |  |
|---|---|---|---|
| | *Warlock* | 1968 | *Anzio* |
| 1962 | *Walk on the Wild Side* | | *Shalako* |
| 1964 | *The Carpetbaggers* | 1972 | *Bluebeard* |
| | *Where Love Has Gone* | 1975 | *The Human Factor* |
| 1965 | *Mirage* | 1976 | *He is My Brother* |
| 1966 | *Alvarez Kelly* | 1979 | *Not Only Strangers* |

## JOHN FRANKENHEIMER

John Michael Frankenheimer was born in 1930 in New York, and gained his first practical experience of the movies in the US Air Force's Motion Picture Squadron. On his discharge he got a job in television, working for CBS as a cameraman, and for a long time, even after he'd started directing movies, live television was where his true loyalties lay; throughout his career he continued to make TV movies. His work as a cameraman stood him in good stead as a director; his movies are noted for their innovative camera angles and techniques. He died in Los Angeles in 2002.

### Select Filmography

| | | | |
|---|---|---|---|
| 1956 | *The Ninth Day* | 1973 | *Story of a Love Story,* |
| 1957 | *The Comedian* | | vt *Impossible Object* |
| | *The Young Stranger* | | *The Iceman Cometh* |
| 1959 | *The Turn of the Screw* | 1974 | *99 and 44/100% Dead,* |
| 1960 | *The Fifth Column* | | vt *Call Harry Crown* |
| 1961 | *The Young Savages* | 1975 | *French Connection II* |
| 1962 | *All Fall Down* | 1977 | *Black Sunday* |
| | *Birdman of Alcatraz* | 1979 | *Prophecy* |
| | *The Manchurian* | 1982 | *The Challenge,* vt *Equals,* |
| | *Candidate* | | vt *Sword of the Ninja* |
| 1964 | *Seven Days in May* | | *The Rainmaker* |
| | *The Train* | 1985 | *The Holcroft Covenant* |
| 1966 | *Grand Prix* | 1986 | *52 Pick-Up* |
| | *Seconds* | 1987 | *Riviera* (as Alan Smithee) |
| 1968 | *The Fixer* | 1989 | *Dead Bang* |
| 1969 | *The Extraordinary* | 1990 | *The Fourth War* |
| | *Seaman* | 1991 | *Year of the Gun* |
| | *The Gypsy Moths* | 1994 | *Against the Wall* |
| 1970l | *Walk the Line* | | *The Burning Season* |
| 1971 | *The Horsemen* | 1996 | *Andersonville* |
| | | | *The Island of Dr Moreau* |

| 1997 | George Wallace | 2001 | The Hire: Ambush |
| 1998 | Ronin | 2002 | Path to War |
| 2000 | Reindeer Games, vt Deception | | |

 **STEPHEN FREARS**

Born in Leicester, UK, in 1941, Stephen Frears did much work in UK television before breaking into the cinema, his breakthrough movie being 1985's *My Beautiful Laundrette*. For some years he directed a string of major movies for Hollywood, including *The Grifters* (1990), *Hero* (1992) and the much-underestimated *Mary Reilly* (1996). More recently he has largely returned to his roots, with smaller-budget movies (some for TV) like the excellent London-set neo-*noir* movie *Dirty Pretty Things* (2002).

## Select Filmography

| 1968 | The Burning |
| 1971 | Gumshoe |
| 1972 | A Day Out |
| 1975 | Daft as a Brush |
| | Sunset Across the Bay |
| | Three Men in a Boat |
| 1976 | Early Struggles |
| | Last Summer |
| | Play Things |
| 1977 | Able's Will |
| 1978 | A Visit from Miss Protheroe |
| | Doris and Doreen |
| | Me! I'm Afraid of Virginia Woolf |
| 1979 | Afternoon Off |
| | Bloody Kids, vt One Joke Too Many |
| | Long Distance Information |
| | One Fine Day |
| 1981 | Going Gently |
| 1982 | Walter |
| 1983 | Saigon: Year of the Cat |
| 1983 | Walter and June |
| 1984 | December Flower |
| | The Hit |
| 1985 | My Beautiful Launderette |
| 1987 | Prick Up Your Ears |
| | Sammy and Rosie Get Laid, vt Sammy and Rosie |
| 1988 | Dangerous Liaisons |
| 1990 | The Grifters |
| 1992 | Hero, vt Accidental Hero |
| 1993 | The Snapper |
| 1996 | Mary Reilly |
| | The Van |
| 1998 | The Hi-Lo Country |
| 2000 | Fail Safe |
| | High Fidelity |
| | Liam |
| 2002 | Dirty Pretty Things |
| 2003 | The Deal |
| 2005 | Mrs Henderson Presents |
| | The Queen |

#  JEAN-LUC GODARD

Born in Paris in 1930, Godard became a naturalized Swiss citizen during WWII, returning to Paris in 1948. His interest in the movies began in the late 1940s/early 1950s; during this period, and later, he wrote a number of significant articles for the celebrated journal *Les Cahiers du Cinéma*, and became a noted member of the *Nouvelle Vague*. His first movie of note was 1959's *Charlotte et Véronique*; his first to win him the international acclaim he still attracts was his 1960 *noir* movie *À Bout de Souffle* (vt *Breathless*).

## Select Filmography

1955    *Une Femme Coquette*
1959    *Charlotte et Véronique, ou Tous les Garçons s'Appellent Patrick*,
        vt *All the Boys Are Called Patrick*
1960    *Charlotte et son Jules*, vt *Charlotte and her Boyfriend*,
        vt *Charlotte and her Jules*
        *À Bout de Souffle*, vt *Breathless*
1961    *Une Femme est une Femme*, vt *A Woman is a Woman*
1962    *Vivre sa Vie: Film en Douze Tableaux*, vt *It's My Life*,
        vt *My Life to Live*
1963    *Carabiniers, Les*, vt *The Carabineers*, vt *The Riflemen*,
        vt *The Soldiers*
        *Le Mépris*, vt *Contempt*
        *Le Petit Soldat*, vt *The Little Soldier*
1964    *Bande à Part*, vt *Band of Outsiders*, vt *The Outsiders*
        *Reportage sur Orly*
        *Une Femme Mariée: Suite de Fragments d'un Film Tourné en*
        *1964*, vt *A Married Woman*
1965    *Alphaville: Une Étrange Aventure de Lemmy Caution*, vt *Alphaville:*
        *A Strange Adventure of Lemmy Caution?*
        *Pierrot le Fou*, vt *Crazy Pete*, vt *Pierrot Goes Wild*
1966    *Made in USA*
        *Masculin, Féminin: 15 Faits Précis*, vt *Masculine, Feminine: In 15 Acts*
1967    *2 ou 3 Choses que Je Sais d'Elle*, vt *Two or Three Things I Know*
        *About Her*
        *La Chinoise, ou Plutôt à la Chinoise: Un Film en Train de se Faire*
        *Week End*, vt *Week-End*, vt *Le Week-end*
1968    *Cinétracts*

Sympathy for the Devil, vt One Plus One
Un Film Comme les Autres, vt A Film Like Any Other, vt A Movie
    like Any Other

1969   Le Gai Savoir, vt Joy of Learning, vt Joyful Wisdom,
        vt The Joy of Knowledge

1970   British Sounds, vt See You at Mao
       Le Vent d'Est, vt East Wind, vt Wind from the East
       Pravda
       Vladimir et Rosa, vt Vladimir and Rosa

1971   Lotte in Italia, vt Struggle in Italy

1972   Letter to Jane, vt Lettre à Jane
       One P.M., vt One A.M./One American Movie, vt One P.M./One
          Parallel Movie
       Tout Va Bien, vt All's Well, vt Just Great

1975   Numéro Deux, vt Number Two

1976   Ici et Ailleurs, vt Here and Elsewhere

1978   Comment ça Va?, vt How is it Going?

1980   Sauve qui Peut (la Vie), vt Every Man for Himself, vt Slow Motion

1981   Lettre à Freddy Buache

1982   Passion, vt Godard's Passion

1983   Prénom Carmen, vt First Name Carmen

1984   Série Noire (TV series)

1985   Je Vous Salue, Marie, vt Hail Mary
       Détective

1986   Grandeur et Décadence, d'un Petit Commerce de Cinéma, la
       Recherche des Acteurs
       Soft and Hard, vt Soft Conversation on Hard Subjects

1987   King Lear
       Soigne ta Droite, vt Keep Up Your Right

1988   On s'est Tous Défilé
       Puissance de la Parole, vt The Power of Speech

1989   Le Rapport Darty

1990   Nouvelle Vague, vt New Wave

1991   Allemagne 90 Neuf Zéro, vt Germany Year 90 Nine Zero

1993   Hélas pour Moi, vt Alas for Me, vt Oh, Woe Is Me
       Les Enfants Jouent à la Russie, vt The Kids Play Russian

1995   Deux Fois Cinquante Ans de Cinéma Français, vt 2 x 50 Years of
         French Cinema, vt Twice Fifty Years of French Cinema
       JLG/JLG – Autoportrait de Décembre, vt JLG/JLG – Self-Portrait in
         December

1996    *For Ever Mozart*
1998    *The Old Place*
2000    *L'Origine du XXIème Siècle*, vt *Origins of the 21st Century*
2001    *Éloge de l'Amour*, vt *In Praise of Love*
2004    *Notre Musique*, vt *Our Music*

##  ALFRED HITCHCOCK

Alfred Joseph Hitchcock was born in London's East End in 1899. His first job in the movies was as a junior film technician; by 1925 he was directing. His early classics in the UK included *The Thirty-Nine Steps* (1935) and *The Lady Vanishes* (1938). Having gained prominence during the 1930s in his homeland, he moved to Hollywood at the turn of the decade and thereafter made a long succession of hit movies, generally psychological thrillers, many of them *noir*. His movie *Psycho* (1960) is often regarded as having sounded the death-knell for *noir*'s classic period, since it spends its first one-third or so riffing on *noir* tropes before becoming something else entirely. He won a Lifetime Achievement Oscar — remarkably, his solitary Oscar — in 1979. In 1980 he was made a Knight Commander of the British Empire. Only a few months later, he died in Los Angeles. His directorial "trademark" was that he appeared briefly — even if only as a newspaper photograph — in all his movies.

### Select Filmography

1925    *The Pleasure Garden*
1926    *The Mountain Eagle*,
            vt *Fear o' God*
1927    *Downhill*, vt *When Boys
            Leave Home*
        *The Lodger*, vt *The Case
            of Jonathan Drew*
        *The Ring*
1928    *Champagne*
        *Easy Virtue*
        *The Farmer's Wife*
1929    *Blackmail*

1929    *The Manxman*
1930    *An Elastic Affair*
        *Murder!*
1930    *Juno and the Paycock*,
            vt *The Shame of Mary
            Boyle*
1931    *Mary*
        *Rich and Strange*,
            vt *East of Shanghai*
        *The Skin Game*
1932    *Number Seventeen*, vt
            *Number 17*
1933    *Waltzes from Vienna*, vt
            *Strauss' Great Waltz*

| | | | |
|---|---|---|---|
| 1934 | The Man Who Knew Too Much | 1947 | The Paradine Case |
| 1935 | The Thirty-Nine Steps | 1948 | Rope |
| 1936 | Sabotage, vt A Woman Alone, vt I Married a Murderer, vt The Hidden Power | 1949 | Under Capricorn |
| | | 1950 | Stage Fright |
| | | 1951 | Strangers on a Train |
| | | 1953 | I Confess |
| | Secret Agent | 1954 | Dial M for Murder |
| 1937 | Young and Innocent, vt The Girl Was Young | | Rear Window |
| | | 1955 | The Trouble with Harry |
| 1938 | The Lady Vanishes | | To Catch a Thief |
| 1939 | Jamaica Inn | 1956 | The Man Who Knew Too Much |
| 1940 | Foreign Correspondent | | |
| | Rebecca | | The Wrong Man |
| 1941 | Mr & Mrs Smith | 1958 | Vertigo |
| | Suspicion | 1959 | North by Northwest |
| 1942 | Saboteur | 1960 | Psycho |
| 1943 | Shadow of a Doubt | 1963 | The Birds |
| 1944 | Madagascar Landing | 1964 | Marnie |
| | Bon Voyage | 1966 | Torn Curtain |
| | Lifeboat | 1969 | Topaz |
| 1945 | Spellbound | 1972 | Frenzy |
| 1946 | Notorious | 1976 | Family Plot |

## JOHN HUSTON

John Marcellus Huston was born in Nevada, Missouri, in 1906; his father was the actor Walter Huston. He had a mixed career before going to Hollywood in the late 1920s, beginning there as an actor and screenwriter. His first movie as a director was *The Maltese Falcon* (1941). In the last decade of his life he became almost better known as an actor than as a director, his performance in Roman Polanski's *Chinatown* (1974) earning him an Oscar nomination. He became an Irish citizen in 1964. He died in 1987 in Middletown, Rhode Island.

### Select Filmography

| | | | |
|---|---|---|---|
| 1941 | The Maltese Falcon | 1946 | Let There Be Light |
| 1942 | Across the Pacific | 1948 | Key Largo |
| | In This Our Life | 1948 | The Treasure of the Sierra Madre |

| | | | |
|---|---|---|---|
| 1949 | We Were Strangers | 1967 | Reflections in a Golden Eye |
| 1950 | The Asphalt Jungle | 1969 | A Walk with Love and Death |
| 1951 | The African Queen | | |
| | The Red Badge of Courage | 1969 | Sinful Davey |
| 1952 | Moulin Rouge | 1970 | The Kremlin Letter |
| 1953 | Beat the Devil | 1972 | Fat City |
| 1956 | Moby Dick | | The Life and Times of Judge Roy Bean |
| 1957 | Heaven Knows, Mr Allison | | |
| 1958 | The Barbarian and the Geisha | 1973 | The Mackintosh Man |
| | | 1975 | The Man Who Would Be King |
| | The Roots of Heaven | | |
| 1960 | The Unforgiven | 1976 | Independence |
| 1961 | The Misfits | 1979 | Love and Bullets |
| 1962 | Freud, vt Freud: The Secret Passion | | Wise Blood |
| | | 1980 | Phobia |
| 1963 | The List of Adrian Messenger | 1981 | Victory, vt Escape to Victory |
| 1964 | The Night of the Iguana | 1982 | Annie |
| 1966 | The Bible . . . In the Beginning | 1984 | Under the Volcano |
| | | 1985 | Prizzi's Honor |
| 1967 | Casino Royale | 1987 | The Dead |

##  FRITZ LANG

Born in Vienna in 1890, Fritz Lang joined the Delta Film Company in 1919, and was soon directing. Of his early movies, the best-known are his two *Dr Mabuse* movies (1922 and 1933; he made a third in 1960, his last movie) and *Metropolis* (1927), a futuristic epic. In 1933 *Das Testament des Dr Mabuse* was banned by the Nazis, yet a few days later Goebbels offered Lang a post heading the German film industry; Lang listened politely, and that night fled to Paris, leaving behind his wife, Thea von Harbou, herself a significant moviemaker and happy to cooperate with the Nazi propaganda machine. Reaching the US, Lang became best-known as a director of crime movies, in particular *noirs*. His output was prolific through the 1930s, 1940s and 1950s, but his reputation spread as someone difficult to work with. By the mid-1950s his Hollywood career was over; his last three movies were made in Germany. A naturalized US citizen, he died in Los Angeles in 1976.

## Select Filmography

1919    *Der goldene See*
        *Der Herr der Liebe*, vt *Master of Love*
        *Die Pest in Florenz*, vt *The Plague in Florence*
        *Halbblut*, vt *The Half-Caste*
        *Harakiri*, vt *Madame Butterfly*
1920    *Das Brillantenschiff*
        *Das wandernde Bild*, vt *The Moving Image*, vt *The Wandering Image*
1921    *Der müde Tod*, vt *Between Two Worlds*, vt *Between Worlds*, vt
            *Beyond the Wall*, vt *Destiny*, vt *The Three Lights*, vt *The
            Weary Death*
        *Vier um die Frau*, vt *Four Around a Woman*, vt *Struggling Hearts*
1922    *Dr Mabuse, der Spieler*, vt *Dr Mabuse, King of Crime*, vt *Dr
            Mabuse: The Gambler*
1924    *Die Nibelungen: Siegfried*, vt *Siegfried*, vt *Siegfried's Death*
        *Die Nibelungen: Kriemhilds Rache*, vt *Die Nibelungen: Kriemhild's
            Revenge*
1927    *Metropolis*
1928    *Spione*, vt *Spies*, vt *The Spy*
1929    *Frau im Mond*, vt *By Rocket to the Moon*, vt *Girl in the Moon*, vt
            *Woman in the Moon*
1931    *M*, vt *The Murderers Are Among Us*
1933    *Das Testament des Dr Mabuse*,
            vt *Dr Mabuse's Testament*, vt *The
            Crimes of Dr Mabuse*, vt *The
            Testament of Dr Mabuse*,
            vt *The Last Will of Dr Mabuse*
1934    *Liliom*
1936    *Fury*
1937    *You Only Live Once*
1938    *You and Me*
1940    *The Return of Frank James*
1941    *Confirm or Deny* (uncredited)
        *Man Hunt*
        *Western Union*
1942    *Moontide* (uncredited)
1943    *Hangmen Also Die*, vt *Hangmen Also Die!*, vt *Lest We Forget*
1944    *Ministry of Fear*
1945    *Scarlet Street*
        *The Woman in the Window*
1946    *Cloak and Dagger*

1948   *Secret Beyond the Door . . .*
1950   *American Guerrilla in the Philippines*, vt *I Shall Return*
       *House by the River*
1952   *Clash by Night*
       *Rancho Notorious*
1953   *The Big Heat*
       *The Blue Gardenia*
1954   *Human Desire*
1955   *Moonfleet*
1956   *Beyond a Reasonable Doubt*
       *While the City Sleeps*
1959   *Das indische Grabmal*, vt *The Indian Tomb*
       *Der Tiger von Eschnapur*, vt *Tiger of Bengal*, vt *Journey to the
           Lost City*
1960   *Die Tausend Augen des Dr Mabuse*, vt *Diabolical Dr Mabuse*, vt
           *Eyes of Evil*, vt *The Shadow vs. the Thousand Eyes of Dr
           Mabuse*, vt *The Thousand Eyes of Dr Mabuse*

 **ANATOLE LITVAK**

Born as Michael Anatole Litwak in Kiev in 1902, Litvak got his first
job in the movies in Russia in 1923, but within a couple of years
had moved to Germany, where he made a number of movies
before fleeing from the Nazis to the UK and then France, where
he made more movies before fleeing once more, this time to
Hollywood, in 1937, there earning a reputation for his broody,
atmospheric crime movies. After the WWII years, which he spent
largely contributing to the propaganda effort, he returned to
crime movies, among others. From the mid-1950s he was working as much in France as in the US. He died in Neuilly-sur-Seine,
France, in 1974.

## Select Filmography
1925   *Tatiana*, vt *Hearts and Dollars*
1930   *Dolly macht Karriere*, vt *Dolly Gets Ahead*, vt *Dolly's Way to
           Stardom*
1931   *Nie wieder Liebe*, vt *No More Love*
1932   *Coeur de Lilas*, vt *Lilac*
       *La Chanson d'une Nuit*, vt *The Song of Night*
       *Tell Me Tonight*, vt *Be Mine Tonight*

| 1933 | *Cette Vieille Canaille*, vt *The Old Devil* |
| | *Sleeping Car*, vt *Love and Let Love* |
| 1935 | *L'Équipage*, vt *Flight into Darkness* |
| 1936 | *Mayerling* |
| 1937 | *The Woman I Love*, vt *The Woman Between* |
| | *Tovarich* |
| 1938 | *The Amazing Dr Clitterhouse* |
| | *The Sisters* |
| 1939 | *Confessions of a Nazi Spy* |
| 1940 | *'Til We Meet Again* |
| | *All This, and Heaven Too* |
| | *Castle on the Hudson*, vt *Years Without Days* |
| | *City for Conquest* |
| 1941 | *Blues in the Night* |
| | *Out of the Fog* |
| 1942 | *This Above All* |
| 1947 | *The Long Night* |
| 1948 | *Sorry, Wrong Number* |
| | *The Snake Pit* |
| 1951 | *Decision Before Dawn* |
| 1953 | *Un Acte d'Amour*, vt *Act of Love* |
| 1955 | *The Deep Blue Sea* |
| 1956 | *Anastasia* |
| 1959 | *The Journey* |
| 1961 | *Aimez-Vous Brahms?*, vt *Goodbye Again* |
| 1962 | *Le Couteau dans la Plaie*, vt *Five Miles to Midnight* |
| 1967 | *La Nuit des Généraux*, vt *The Night of the Generals* |
| 1970 | *La Dame dans l'Auto avec des Lunettes et un Fusil*, vt *The Lady in the Car with Glasses and a Gun* |

## DAVID LYNCH

Born in 1946 in Missoula, Montana, David Keith Lynch made a number of shorts before his first feature, *Eraserhead* (1977), shot him to prominence. The mainstream lured him for his next two features, *The Elephant Man* (1980) and *Dune* (1984), but the disaster of the latter fortunately turned him back to doing what he does best: making David Lynch movies, almost all of which are deeply infused with *noir* sensibilities – as example his internationally successful 1990–91 TV series *Twin Peaks*.

His daughter, Jennifer Chambers Lynch, has directed the very dad-like movie *Boxing Helena* (1993).

**Select Filmography**

| | |
|---|---|
| 1968: | The Alphabet |
| 1970: | The Grandmother |
| 1974: | The Amputee |
| 1977: | Eraserhead |
| 1980: | The Elephant Man |
| 1984: | Dune |
| 1986: | Blue Velvet |
| 1990: | Twin Peaks (TV movie) |
| 1990: | Wild at Heart |
| 1992: | Twin Peaks: Fire Walk with Me, vt Fire Walk with Me |
| 1997: | Lost Highway |
| 1999: | The Straight Story |
| 2001: | Mulholland Drive |
| 2002: | Darkened Room |
| 2002: | Does That Hurt You? |
| 2002: | Rabbits |

## JEAN-PIERRE MELVILLE

Born Jean-Pierre Grumbach in 1917 in Paris, Melville took his *nom de film* from the pseudonym he used in the French Resistance during WWII. In 1946 he set up a movie production house, his debut feature being the war movie *Le Silence de la Mer* (1947), which can be regarded as a *noir* movie in all but genre. He collaborated with Cocteau on *Les Enfants Terrible* (1949), and then in 1955 made the classic *Bob le Flambeau*; thereafter his career never looked back, as he created a string of excellent *noirs* and thrillers. He also acted occasionally in his own and other directors' movies; among the latter were Jean-Luc Godard's *À Bout de Souffle* (1960) and Claude Chabrol's *Landru* (1963). He died in Paris in 1973.

**Select Filmography**

1945    Vingt-Quatre Heures de la Vie d'un Clown
1947    Le Silence de la Mer
1949    Les Enfants Terribles, vt The Strange Ones
1953    Quand tu Liras cette Lettre, vt When You Read this Letter
1955    Bob le Flambeur, vt Bob the Gambler, vt Fever Heat
1959    Deux Hommes dans Manhattan, vt Two Men in Manhattan
1961    Léon Morin, Prêtre, vt Leon Morin, Priest, vt The Forgiven Sinner
1962    Le Doulos, vt Doulos: The Finger Man, vt The Finger Man
1963    L'Aîné des Ferchaux, vt Magnet of Doom
1966    Le Deuxième Souffle, vt Second Breath
1967    Le Samouraï, vt The Godson
1969    L'Armée des Ombres, vt Army in the Shadows, vt The Shadow Army
1970    Le Cercle Rouge, vt The Red Circle
1972    Un Flic, vt Dirty Money

##  NICHOLAS RAY

Raymond Nicholas Kienzle, born in Galesville, Wisconsin, in 1911, took on the name Nick Ray in 1931. After working in the theatre during the 1930s, he spent much of the WWII years in radio assisting the wartime propaganda machine. His first job in the movies was assisting on Elia Kazan's *A Tree Grows in Brooklyn* (1945). His directorial debut was for RKO in 1949, with *They Live by Night*. He then directed a string of *noirs* and other movies for RKO until becoming freelance in 1953; of these, *In a Lonely Place* (1950) is perhaps most notable. In 1955 he made *Rebel Without a Cause*, undoubtedly his single best-known movie. He died in 1979 in New York.

### Select Filmography

| | |
|---|---|
| 1949 | *A Woman's Secret* |
| | *Knock on Any Door* |
| | *Roseanna McCoy* |
| | *They Live by Night*, vt *The Twisted Road* |
| 1950 | *Born to Be Bad* |
| | *In a Lonely Place* |
| 1951 | *Flying Leathernecks* |
| | *The Racket* |
| 1952 | *Androcles and the Lion* |
| | *Macao* |
| | *On Dangerous Ground* |
| | *The Lusty Men* |
| 1954 | *Johnny Guitar* |
| 1955 | *Rebel Without a Cause* |
| | *Run for Cover*, vt *Colorado* |
| 1956 | *Bigger Than Life* |
| | *Hot Blood*, vt *Bad Blood* |
| 1957 | *Amère Victoire*, vt *Bitter Victory* |
| | *The True Story of Jesse James*, vt *The James Brothers* |
| 1958 | *Party Girl* |
| | *Wind Across the Everglades* |
| 1959 | *The Savage Innocents* |
| 1961 | *King of Kings* |
| 1963 | *55 Days at Peking* |
| 1975 | *Wet Dreams* |
| 1976 | *We Can't Go Home Again* |
| 1978 | *Marco* |
| 1980 | *Lightning Over Water* |

*"You're not a detective, you're a slot machine.
You'd slit your own throat for 6 bits plus tax!"*
Murder, My Sweet (1944)

##  Robert Siodmak

Born in 1900 in Memphis, Tennessee (his German parents were travelling in the US at the time), Robert Siodmak was the elder brother of screenwriter, novelist and movie director Curt/Kurt Siodmak. He made his early movies in Germany, but the Nazi rise caused him to flee to Paris, whence in 1940 he fled to Hollywood. Initially he worked on B-movies. The success of *Son of Dracula* (1943) brought him the opportunity to direct bigger-budget pictures; thereafter he made several *noirs* as well as near-*noirs* like the gothic melodrama *The Spiral Staircase* (1946). In 1953 he returned to Europe, filming first in France and then in his native Germany. He died in 1973 in Locarno, Switzerland.

### Select Filmography

1930   *Abschied*, vt *Farewell*
          *Der Kampf mit dem Drachen Oder: Die Tragedie des
               Untermieters*
          *Menschen am Sonntag*, vt *People on Sunday*
1931   *Autour d'une Enquéte*
          *Der Mann, der seinen Mörder sucht*, vt *Looking for his Murderer*
          *Voruntersuchung*, vt *Inquest*
1932   *Quick*
          *Stürme der Leidenschaft*, vt *Storms of Passion*, vt *Tempest*
          *Tumultes*
1933   *Brennendes Geheimnis*, vt *The Burning Secret*
          *Le Sexe Faible*, vt *Weaker Sex*
1936   *La Vie Parisienne*, vt *The Parisian Life*
          *Le Grand Refrain*, vt *Symphonie D'Amour*
          *Mister Flow*, vt *Compliments of Mr Flow*
1937   *Cargaison Blanche*, vt *Traffic in Souls*, vt *Woman Racket*
1938   *Mollenard*, vt *Hatred*
          *Ultimatum*
1939   *Pièges*, vt *Personal Column*, vt *Snares*
1941   *West Point Widow*
1942   *Fly-By-Night*, vt *Secrets of G32*
          *My Heart Belongs to Daddy*
          *The Night Before the Divorce*
1943   *Someone to Remember*, vt *Gallant Thoroughbred*
          *Son of Dracula*
1944   *Christmas Holiday*
          *Cobra Woman*

1944  *Phantom Lady*
      *The Suspect*
1945  *The Strange Affair of Uncle Harry*, vt *Guilty of Murder?*,
          vt *Uncle Harry*
1946  *The Dark Mirror*
      *The Killers*, vt *A Man Alone*
      *The Spiral Staircase*
1947  *Time Out of Mind*
1948  *Cry of the City*
1949  *Criss Cross*
      *The Great Sinner*
1950  *Deported*
      *The File on Thelma Jordon*, vt *Thelma Jordon*
1951  *The Whistle at Eaton Falls*, vt *Richer than the Earth*
1952  *The Crimson Pirate*
1954  *Le Grand Jeu*, vt *Card of Fate*, vt *Flesh and the Woman*
1955  *Die Ratten*, vt *The Rats*
1956  *Mein Vater, der Schauspieler*
1957  *Nachts, wenn der Teufel kam*, vt *Nights, When the Devil Came*,
          vt *The Devil Strikes at Night*
1958  *Dorothea Angermann*
1959  *Katia*, vt *Adorable Sinner*, vt *Magnificent Sinner*
      *The Rough and the Smooth*, vt *Portrait of a Sinner*
1960  *Mein Schulfreund*, vt *My School Chum*
1961  *L'Affaire Nina B.*, vt *The Nina B. Affair*
1962  *Escape from East Berlin*, vt *Tunnel 28*
1964  *Der Schut*, vt *The Shoot*, vt *Yellow Devil*
1965  *Die Pyramide des Sonnengottes*, vt *Pyramid of the Sun God*
      *Der Schatz der Azteken*, vt *The Treasure of the Aztecs*
1967  *Custer of the West*, vt *Custer, Homme de l'Ouest*
1968  *Kampf um Rom I*, vt *Struggle for Rome*, vt *The Fight for Rome*, vt
          *The Last Roman*
1969  *Kampf um Rom II – Der Verrat*

## JACQUES TOURNEUR

Born in 1904 in Paris, Jacques Tourneur became a permanent US resident at the age of 10. His father was director Maurice Tourneur, so young Jacques's first jobs in the movies were in the US assisting dad. When the family returned to France in 1928, Jacques went too, graduating to the directorial chair in 1931. In

1935 he returned to Hollywood. In 1942 Val Lewton set up his B-movie division and RKO commissioned Tourneur to direct the first two offerings, *Cat People* (1942) and *I Walked with a Zombie* (1943); these were successful, and RKO gave Tourneur higher-budget pictures to direct. He died in 1977 in Bergerac, France.

## Select Filmography

1931    *Tout Ça ne Vaut pas l'Amour*
       *Un Vieux Garçon*
1933    *Pour Être Aimé*
       *Toto*
1934    *Les Filles de la Concierge*
1936    *Killer-Dog*
       *Master Will Shakespeare*
       *The Jonker Diamond*
1937    *The Boss Didn't Say Good Morning*
       *The Grand Bounce*
       *The King Without a Crown*
       *The Man in the Barn*
       *The Rainbow Pass*
1938    *Strange Glory*
       *The Face Behind the Mask*
       *The Ship That Died*
       *Think It Over*
1939    *Nick Carter, Master Detective*
       *They All Come Out*
       *Yankee Doodle Goes to Town*
1940    *Phantom Raiders*, vt *Nick Carter in Panama*
1941    *Doctors Don't Tell*
1942    *Cat People*
       *The Incredible Stranger*
       *The Magic Alphabet*
1943    *I Walked with a Zombie*
       *The Leopard Man*
1944    *Days of Glory*
       *Experiment Perilous*
1946    *Canyon Passage*

1947    *Out of the Past*, vt *Build My Gallows High*
1948    *Berlin Express*
1949    *Easy Living*
1950    *Stars in My Crown*
       *The Flame and the Arrow*
1951    *Anne of the Indies*
       *Circle of Danger*
1952    *Way of a Gaucho*
1953    *Appointment in Honduras*, vt *Jungle Fury*
1955    *Stranger on Horseback*
       *Wichita*
1956    *Great Day in the Morning*
1957    *Night of the Demon*, vt *Curse of the Demon*, vt *Haunted*
       *Nightfall*
1958    *The Fearmakers*
       *Cool and Lam*
1959    *Giant of Marathon*
       *Frontier Rangers*
       *Mission of Danger*
       *Timbuktu*
1960    *Aftermath*, vt *The Code of Jonathan West*
       *The Barbara Stanwyck Show* (TV series)
1961    *Fury River*
1964    *The Comedy of Terrors*, vt *The Graveside Story*
1965    *The City Under the Sea*, vt *City in the Sea*, vt *War-Gods of the Deep*

##  RAOUL WALSH

Albert Edward Walsh was born in New York in 1887 and, after running away from home in his youth, had an adventurous life before becoming first a stage and then a screen actor. He shot a whole string of movies during the 1910s and 1920s that made him one of Hollywood's front-line directors; best-known today is *The Thief of Bagdad* (1924). In the late 1930s he moved to Warner, where it was primarily because of his importance as a director that he became involved in *noir*: stars there included James Cagney and Humphrey Bogart. He retired in 1964 because of deteriorating vision in his remaining eye – he'd lost the other while filming *In Old Arizona* (1929) – and died in 1980 in Simi Valley, California.

### Select Filmography

1919 *Evangeline*
*Should a Husband Forgive?*
1920 *From Now On*
*The Deep Purple*
*The Strongest*
1921 *Serenade*
*The Oath*
1922 *Kindred of the Dust*
1923 *Lost and Found on a South Sea Island*, vt *Captain Blackbird*, vt *Passion of the Sea*, vt *Lost and Found*
*Rosita*
1924 *The Thief of Bagdad*
1925 *East of Suez*
*The Spaniard*, vt *Spanish Love*
*The Wanderer*
1926 *The Lady of the Harem*
*The Lucky Lady*
*What Price Glory*
1927 *The Loves of Carmen*
*The Monkey Talks*
1928 *In Old Arizona*
*Me, Gangster*

1928 *Sadie Thompson*
*The Red Dance*, vt *The Red Dancer of Moscow*
1929 *Hot for Paris*
*The Cock-Eyed World*, vt *The Cockeyed World*
1930 *The Big Trail*
1931 *The Man Who Came Back*
*The Yellow Ticket*, vt *The Yellow Passport*
*Women of All Nations*
1932 *Me and My Gal*
*Wild Girl*, vt *Salomy Jane*
1933 *The Bowery*
1935 *Baby Face Harrington*
*Every Night at Eight*
*Under Pressure*
1936 *Big Brown Eyes*
*Klondike Annie*
*Spendthrift*
1937 *Artists and Models*
*Hitting a New High*
*Jump for Glory*, vt *When Thief Meets Thief*
*OHMS*, vt *You're in the Army Now*

1938  *College Swing*, vt *Swing,*
          *Teacher, Swing*
1939  *St Louis Blues*, vt *Best of*
          *the Blues*
      *The Roaring Twenties*
1940  *Dark Command*
      *They Drive by Night,*
          vt *The Road to Frisco*
1941  *High Sierra*
      *Manpower*
      *The Strawberry Blonde*
      *They Died with Their Boots On*
1942  *Desperate Journey*
      *Gentleman Jim*
1943  *Action in the North Atlantic*
      *Background to Danger*
      *Northern Pursuit*
1944  *Uncertain Glory*
1945  *Objective, Burma!*, vt
          *Operation Burma*
      *Salty O'Rourke*
      *San Antonio*
      *The Horn Blows at Midnight*
1947  *Cheyenne*, vt *The Wyoming*
          *Kid*
      *Pursued*
      *Stallion Road*
      *The Man I Love*
1948  *Fighter Squadron*
      *One Sunday Afternoon*
      *Silver River*
1949  *Colorado Territory*, vt *North*
          *of the Rio Grande*
1949  *White Heat*
1950  *Montana*
1951  *Along the Great Divide,*
          vt *The Travelers*
      *Captain Horatio*
          *Hornblower RN,*
          vt *Captain Horatio*
          *Hornblower*

1951  *Distant Drums*
      *The Enforcer*, vt *Murder,*
          *Inc.*
1952  *Blackbeard, the Pirate*
      *Glory Alley*
      *The World in His Arms*
1953  *A Lion Is in the Streets*
      *Gun Fury*
      *Sea Devils*
      *The Lawless Breed*
1954  *Saskatchewan*, vt *O'Rourke*
          *of the Royal Mounted*
1955  *Battle Cry*
      *The Tall Men*
1956  *The King and Four Queens*
      *The Revolt of Mamie Stover*
1957  *Band of Angels*
1958  *The Naked and the Dead*
      *The Sheriff of Fractured Jaw*
1959  *A Private's Affair*
1960  *Esther and the King*
1961  *Marines, Let's Go*
1964  *A Distant Trumpet*

##  ORSON WELLES

Born in Kenosha, Wisconsin, in 1915, George Orson Welles was orphaned by age 12 with an inheritance sufficient to allow him to do much as he wanted. He and John Houseman set up the Federal Theatre Project, which led to the Mercury Theater, whose radio players, under Welles's direction, produced plays including the famous 1938 adaptation of H.G. Wells's 1898 novel *The War of the Worlds*. His first movie of note was *Citizen Kane* (1941) for RKO; he directed, co-wrote, starred and produced. It made a loss at the time, since William Randolph Hearst — the original for Citizen Kane — ensured all his newspapers boycotted the least mention of its name. Welles's next movie, *The Magnificent Ambersons* (1942), made an even greater loss, and RKO fired him. Thereafter he made as many movies in Europe as in Hollywood. His *noir* movie *Touch of Evil* (1958) was exceptional, even though butchered by Universal–International before release. (A "restored" version was produced in the late 1990s.) Also extraordinary are his *noir*-like adaptation *Le Procès* (1963; vt *The Trial*) of the 1925 Franz Kafka novel, and his performance as Harry Lime in *The Third Man* (1949), for which he also wrote his own scenes. He died in 1985 in Hollywood.

**Select Filmography**

1934  *The Hearts of Age*
1938  *Too Much Johnson*
1941  *Citizen Kane*
1942  *The Magnificent Ambersons*
1944  *Journey Into Fear*
1946  *The Stranger*
1947  *The Lady from Shanghai*
1948  *Macbeth*
1952  *The Tragedy of Othello: The Moor of Venice*, vt *Othello*
1955  *Mr Arkadin*, vt *Confidential Report*
1958  *The Fountain of Youth*
      *Touch of Evil*
1962  *Le Procès*, vt *The Trial*
1965  *Campanadas a Medianoche*, vt *Chimes at Midnight*, vt *Falstaff*
1968  *The Immortal Story*
      *Vienna*
1969  *The Merchant of Venice*
1970  *The Deep*
1971  *London*
1972  *The Other Side of the Wind*
1974  *Vérités et Mensonges*, vt *F for Fake*

# BILLY WILDER

Born as Samuel Wilder in Sucha, Austria–Hungary, Billy Wilder started in the movies in Germany as a scripter, often for director Robert Siodmak. Fleeing the Nazis, he worked briefly in France – making his directorial debut there – before coming to Hollywood, where he was a successful screenwriter before being given, in 1942, the opportunity to direct. His big breakthrough came with the *noir* classic *Double Indemnity* (1944); *Sunset Boulevard* (1950) was another *noir* highlight. In 1981 he retired from the movies. The American Film Institute gave him its Life Achievement Award in 1986, and in 1988 the Academy followed suit with its Irving G. Thalberg Award. He died in 2002 in Beverly Hills.

## Select Filmography

1934   *Mauvaise Graine*, vt *Bad Blood*, vt *Bad Seed*
1942   *The Major and the Minor*
1943   *Five Graves to Cairo*
1944   *Double Indemnity*
1945   *Death Mills*
       *The Lost Weekend*
1948   *A Foreign Affair*
       *The Emperor Waltz*
1950   *Sunset Boulevard*
1951   *Ace in the Hole*, vt *The Big Carnival*
1953   *Stalag 17*
1954   *Sabrina*, vt *Sabrina Fair*
1955   *The Seven Year Itch*

1957   *Love in the Afternoon*
       *The Spirit of St Louis*
       *Witness for the Prosecution*
1959   *Some Like It Hot*
1960   *The Apartment*
1961   *One, Two, Three*
1963   *Irma la Douce*
1964   *Kiss Me, Stupid*
1966   *The Fortune Cookie*, vt *Meet Whiplash Willie*
1970   *The Private Life of Sherlock Holmes*
1972   *Avanti!*
1974   *The Front Page*
1978   *Fedora*
1981   *Buddy Buddy*

*"I don't think you fully understand, Bigelow.
You've been murdered."*
D.O.A. (1950)

# RAYMOND CHANDLER AND THE MOVIES

Born in 1888 in Chicago, Raymond Thornton Chandler was raised in the UK before returning to the US. After an unsuccessful career as a business executive, he turned to writing for *Black Mask*, believing he could make literature (and a living) out of hardboiled crime fiction. In this he succeeded with his six major novels *The Big Sleep* (1939), *Farewell, My Lovely* (1940), *The High Window* (1942), *The Lady in the Lake* (1943), *The Little Sister* (1949) and *The Long Goodbye* (1953); the later *Playback* (1958) was disappointing. His unfinished novel *Poodle Springs* was completed by Robert B. Parker and published in 1989. All featured private eye Philip Marlowe and all were filmed, some more than once, except *Playback*, although Chandler wrote a screenplay for it. He died in La Jolla, California, in 1959.

Although his relations with Hollywood and its directors were always tense, Chandler also wrote screenplays independent of his novels, two of them for movies that have become unchallenged classics: *Double Indemnity* (1944; coscripted with director Billy Wilder) and *Strangers on a Train* (1951; coscripted with Czenzi Ormonde; dir Alfred Hitchcock). He also wrote the minor classic *The Blue Dahlia* (1946; dir George Marshall).

## FAREWELL, MY LOVELY

Although not Chandler's first novel, this was the first to be filmed ... under a different title and with the central character changed. RKO had a successful detective series based on Michael Arlen's character Gay Lawrence (aka The Falcon); they bought the rights to *Farewell, My Lovely* for $2000 and tailored it to fit the series in *The Falcon Takes Over* (1942), dir Irving Reis, scr Lynn Root and Frank Fenton, with George Sanders in the title role.

The second version, also from RKO (who got two movies for one purchase of the rights), at least stayed relatively faithful to the book and featured Philip Marlowe, but the title was changed because RKO worried the original title might be thought a bodice-ripper. A classic of the genre, *Murder, My Sweet* (1945), dir Edward Dmytryk, scr John Paxton, had Dick Powell as Marlowe. For the UK the movie was sensibly retitled *Farewell, My Lovely*.

Yet more faithful to the novel was *Farewell My Lovely* (1975), dir Dick Richards, scr David Zelag Goodman. This was the first of two movies starring Robert Mitchum as (a rather elderly) Marlowe. Charlotte Rampling was the *femme fatale*.

## THE HIGH WINDOW

There has yet to be a movie version of *The High Window* bearing the novel's own title. The first movie was *Time to Kill* (1942); this suffered the same indignity as the first version of *Farewell, My Lovely*, being jammed into a pre-existing series starring someone else's P.I., here Brett Halliday's hero Mike Shayne. It was dir Herbert I. Leeds, scr Clarence Upson Young, with Lloyd Nolan as Shayne.

*The Brasher Doubloon* (1947; vt *The High Window*), dir John Brahm, scr Dorothy Hannah, was much more impressive; as with RKO's purchase for two versions of *Farewell, My Lovely*, this was the second version 20th Century–Fox made for their single (smallish) outlay. *The Brasher Doubloon* had been Chandler's working title, rejected by the publisher, for *The High Window*. George Montgomery played Marlowe.

## THE BIG SLEEP

This novel was luckier. *The Big Sleep* (1946), dir Howard Hawks, starring Humphrey Bogart and Lauren Bacall, had a script primarily by William Faulkner and Leigh Brackett, with further contributions from Jules Furthman. Bogart and Bacall sizzled together onscreen and off – they'd married the previous year, having fallen in love while making *To Have and Have Not* (1945) together. The delay between the novel's publication and the appearance of the movie occurred because the Hollywood studios were nervous about the novel's "sensationalism" – notably the sex, drugs and pornography in the plot. Eventually Hawks persuaded Warner Bros. to take it on.

The second version, *The Big Sleep* (1978), positively revelled in those aspects, as one might expect from its director, Michael Winner, who also scripted. In this version, the story has been updated to the 1970s and the locale, bizarrely, has shifted to London. Robert Mitchum was Marlowe.

### THE LADY IN THE LAKE

Filming Marlowe stories was all the rage in Hollywood in the late 1940s, with *Murder, My Sweet* in 1945, *The Big Sleep* in 1946 and *The Brasher Doubloon* in 1947. *Lady in the Lake* was also released in 1947; scr Steve Fisher with uncredited contributions from Chandler himself, it stars its director, Robert Montgomery, as Marlowe . . . except that Marlowe himself barely appears on camera. In an attempt to recreate the power of Chandler's first-person narration, Montgomery used the "subjective camera" throughout – which is to say, the camera represented Marlowe's eyes, through which the audience saw the story. Chandler called the technique a "cheap Hollywood trick".

### THE LITTLE SISTER

Over 20 years passed before another Marlowe movie appeared. This novel was filmed in 1969 as *Marlowe*, dir Paul Bogart, scr Stirling Silliphant, with James Garner in the title role of another updated rendering. Ably assisted by Gayle Hunnicutt as glamorous star Mavis Wald, Garner makes a surprisingly good Marlowe, and *Marlowe* a surprisingly good movie. Later Garner essentially reprised Marlowe for the long-running TV series *The Rockford Files* (1974–80).

### THE LONG GOODBYE

The most controversial of all the Marlowe movies, *The Long Goodbye* (1973) dir Robert Altman, scr Leigh Brackett (who had coscripted the classic *The Big Sleep*), starring Elliott Gould as Marlowe, is both loved and hated. Its first New York opening was cancelled because of overwhelmingly negative reactions at the previews; when the movie was relaunched a few months later, Pauline Kael described it as "probably the best American movie ever made that almost didn't open in New York". Many reviewers differed, objecting to Brackett's revamping of the plot and particularly to Gould's portrayal of Marlowe as operating behind a bumblingly good-natured persona.

### POODLE SPRINGS

The TV movie *Poodle Springs* (1998) was dir Bob Rafelson, scr Tom Stoppard, and starred James Caan as one of the better Marlowes. Chandler had written four chapters of this Marlowe tale as *The Poodle Springs Story* before he died; it is set in and around Palm Springs and features a married Marlowe. The novel was completed for him by Robert B. Parker (whose own series hero is a P.I. called Spenser).

### MARLOWE ON TV

There have been two TV series featuring the character. *Philip Marlowe, Detective* ran for 26 episodes in 1959–60 and starred Philip Carey. *Philip Marlowe, Private Eye* ran for five episodes, each based on a Chandler non-Marlowe short story with the detective's identity changed to fit, in 1983; it starred Powers Boothe, with voiceover by Stacy Keach.

# A LIBRARY OF
# CLASSIC-ERA *NOIR*

Any attempt to produce a definitive listing of classic *noir* movies is of course doomed to failure: one of the great joys of the movies is that enjoyment of them is largely a subjective matter, so one person's Top Twenty or Top Fifty is likely to differ radically from another's. What is presented over the next few pages is, then, a selection of movies that, taken together, offer a representative cross-section of the Golden Age of "the American Style".

Contemporaneous *noirs* made outside the US are to be found on pages 73-77.

### CITIZEN KANE
dir Orson Welles, 1941

Hugely influential, this takes the form almost of a biopic as it probes the spiritual corruption of powerful magnate Charles Foster Kane (played by Welles and intended as a portrayal of William Randolph Hearst) as a representative of what is destroying the American Dream; as such, it is a murder mystery, the murder being that not of a man but of a man's soul. This movie established a new benchmark for what could and should be done with the cinematic medium, not least for its visuals, done by Gregg Toland, which can be seen as almost a textbook of *noir*.

### HIGH SIERRA
dir Raoul Walsh, 1941

Gangster Humphrey Bogart is sprung from prison to carry out a heist. *En route*, he falls in love with clubfooted Joan Leslie, to whom he gives money so she may have her condition cured. Among his crew is showgirl Ida Lupino; she is the only other member of the team to survive the getaway after the heist. Cops in pursuit, Bogart makes a play for Leslie, only to discover her heart is elsewhere; so he settles for Lupino instead. Yet tragedy is all the future holds for them.

### THE MALTESE FALCON
dir John Huston, 1941

The third and best movie to be based on the 1930 novel by Dashiell Hammett, this has Humphrey Bogart as Sam Spade and Mary Astor as *femme fatale* Brigid O'Shaugnessy. Trying to find the murderer of his partner, Spade becomes embroiled in the hunt for the Maltese Falcon, a stupendously valuable figurine sought by diverse crooks. (See page 11.)

### I WAKE UP SCREAMING
dir H. Bruce Humberstone, 1941

Actress Carole Landis is murdered, and cop Laird Cregar is intent on sending promoter Victor Mature to the chair for the slaying, even though he admits he believes Mature innocent. Mature hides out with Landis's sister Betty Grable, with whom he is in love.

### DOUBLE INDEMNITY
dir Billy Wilder, 1944

Scr Raymond Chandler with Wilder, based on the 1944 novel by James M. Cain, this tells of insurance salesman Fred MacMurray being seduced by supreme *femme fatale* Barbara Stanwyck into killing her husband so they can share the life-insurance money. The murder done, they find suspicion closing in on them as, in particular, MacMurray's wily boss Edward G. Robinson finds holes in the story.

### MURDER, MY SWEET
dir Edward Dmytryk, 1944

The first genuine cinema adaptation of Raymond Chandler's 1940 novel *Farewell, My Lovely*. Dick Powell, a creditable Marlowe, tackles one of Chandler's typically convoluted plots. (See page 40.)

### DETOUR
dir Edgar G. Ulmer, 1945

Tom Neal is hitchhiking to Hollywood to join his girlfriend when picked up by driver Edmund MacDonald, who tells of a female hitchhiker who recently resisted his advances. Neal takes a turn at driving, then discovers MacDonald, supposedly asleep, is dead. Assuming he'll be thought a murderer, Neal buries the body and drives on. In turn he gives a lift to Ann Savage, the hitchhiker who resisted MacDonald. When he tells his tale she thinks he's a murderer, and tries to blackmail him into bilking MacDonald's heirs. A classic cheapie.

### SCARLET STREET
dir Fritz Lang, 1945

A remake of *La Chienne* (1931) dir Jean Renoir. Meek cashier and amateur painter Edward G. Robinson falls into the clutches of *femme fatale* Joan Bennett. While he schemes to rid himself of his loveless marriage to wed her, she and casually violent spiv boyfriend Dan Duryea discover Robinson's paintings will fetch high prices, and pass them off as hers. Finally discovering her treachery, Robinson slays her; Duryea is executed for the murder. *Scarlet Street* benefits from exquisite plotting as well as outstanding performances and direction.

### THE BIG SLEEP
dir Howard Hawks, 1946

Based on the 1939 novel by Raymond Chandler, this has Humphrey Bogart as Marlowe tackling a complicated case of blackmail and murder. (See page 40.)

### THE BLUE DAHLIA
dir George Marshall, 1946

With an original script by Raymond Chandler, this sees Navy veteran Alan Ladd coming home from the war to find wife Doris Dowling is manifestly unfaithful to him. He is still digesting this when she is murdered, with him the obvious suspect. In tandem with Veronica Lake, and in a plot complicated by blackmailing hotel detective Will Wright, Ladd solves the murder before the cops can grab him.

### FALLEN ANGEL
dir Otto Preminger, 1946

In a small California town, fake medium Dana Andrews falls for local waitress Linda Darnell. He plans to romance rich Alice Faye until he has extracted her money, then marry Darnell. But Darnell is murdered, and Andrews is Suspect #1. Fleeing with Faye, he realizes he loves her.

### THE POSTMAN ALWAYS RINGS TWICE
dir Tay Garnett, 1946

Based on the 1934 James M. Cain novel. Drifter John Garfield arrives at a California diner, and almost immediately he and the owner's wife, Lana Turner, are hot for each other. Turner hatches a scheme to murder her husband, Cecil Kellaway, but Garfield injures himself in so doing. The cops are keen to pin the murder on Turner, and weakly Garfield aids; but the case never comes to trial. Thereafter they marry, which is when the blackmail starts ...

### DARK PASSAGE
dir Delmar Daves, 1947

Falsely convicted of murdering his wife, Humphrey Bogart escapes prison and is "adopted" by beautiful San Francisco artist Lauren Bacall, whose own father was falsely convicted for killing her stepmother. Bogart discovers that one of Bacall's friends (Agnes Moorehead) is the woman whose perjury secured his own conviction. He undergoes facial surgery as disguise, and shows Moorehead is the murderess.

### OUT OF THE PAST
dir Jacques Tourneur, 1947

Once Robert Mitchum was hired by racketeer Kirk Douglas to track down Douglas's mistress Jane Greer, who had run off with $40,000. Mitchum found her in Mexico and they fell in love, but eventually she was revealed as thief and murderer and he fled. Now he finds she has returned to Douglas, who wants to use Mitchum as patsy in another murder plot.

### CALL NORTHSIDE 777
dir Henry Hathaway

Based loosely on a true story. Investigative journalist James Stewart is persuaded by cleaner Kasia Orzazewski that her son Richard Conté, jailed a decade ago for killing a cop, is innocent, and he takes up a crusade to have the case reopened. Despite constant obstacles thrown in his way and the continued false testimony of perjuring witness Betty Garde, Stewart proves his point and Conté is released.

### CRISS CROSS
dir Robert Siodmak, 1948

Payroll guard Burt Lancaster is lured into a tryst by ex-wife Yvonne DeCarlo, now living with gangster Dan Duryea. Caught, the couple claim the sole purpose of their meeting was to plan the heist of a payload Lancaster will be driving. Duryea falls for the lie, which means Lancaster must go through with it.

### SORRY, WRONG NUMBER
dir Anatole Litvak, 1948

Based on a radio play by Lucille Fletcher, who also scripted. Wealthy bedridden wife Barbara Stanwyck overhears a phone conversation in which a woman's murder is being plotted. Trying to track husband Burt Lancaster on the phone, she finds he has motives aplenty to want her dead — yet still, though convinced she's the intended victim, she cannot believe his guilt. Edge-of-the-seat stuff, distinguished by a sophisticated flashbacking narrative technique.

"You're wearing the wrong shade of lipstick, mister."
*The Blue Dahlia* (1946)

### THE ASPHALT JUNGLE
dir John Huston, 1950

Based on the 1949 novel by W.R. Burnett. Criminal mastermind Sam Jaffe and bent lawyer Louis Calhern plan a heist, and Jaffe rounds up a team. But almost as soon as the robbery is done the complications and doublecrossing set in.

### D.O.A.
dir Rudolph Maté, 1950

Edmond O'Brien has been poisoned by crooks involved in illicit iridium dealings; he knows he has only days to live. With the help of fiancée Pamela Britton, he tracks and kills the poisoner, telling the full story to the cops just before he himself dies. Remade unnecessarily as *D.O.A.* (1988), dir Rocky Morton and Annabel Jankel.

### IN A LONELY PLACE
dir Nicholas Ray, 1950

Hollywood screenwriter Humphrey Bogart is a disturbed and sometimes violent man. Accused of murdering hat-check girl Martha Stewart, he is saved from arrest by a witness, comely neighbour Gloria Grahame. Romance blossoms between them, but is increasingly tempered on her part by his paranoid suspicions and outbursts of violence.

### NO WAY OUT
dir Joseph L. Mankiewicz, 1950

Bigot Richard Widmark gets his gangster friends to engineer race riots as a means of avenging the murder of his brother, whom black doctor Sidney Poitier did his unsuccessful best to save. But then Widmark himself is injured, and Poitier, who could save him, must choose between conscience and feelings.

### QUICKSAND
dir Irving Pichel, 1950

Garage mechanic Mickey Rooney pilfers from the till in hopes of impressing pretty Jeanne Cagney (James Cagney's sister). But the auditor arrives unexpectedly, and Rooney must find some way to replace the money. His petty crime thus engenders ever graver ones, culminating in a gunfight with the cops. Outstanding in the supporting cast is Peter Lorre; this was intended as the first in a series of Rooney–Lorre collaborations, but in the event was the only one made.

### SUNSET BOULEVARD
(vt *Sunset Blvd.*)
dir Billy Wilder, 1950
Broke scriptwriter William Holden becomes acolyte to has-been movie star Gloria Swanson, who's convinced her magnificent comeback is only just around the corner. Soon he is having secret trysts with studio reader Nancy Olson as they write a screenplay together. Swanson tries to kill the romance by telling Olson that Holden is just her (Swanson's) toyboy. Standing up to Swanson for once, Holden storms out, but as he does so she murders him. The start of the movie has Holden already dead, his voiceover announcing he will tell how he came to be killed.

### STRANGERS ON A TRAIN
dir Alfred Hitchcock, 1951
Based on the 1950 novel by Patricia Highsmith, this classic *noir* sees Farley Granger bamboozled by Robert Walker, whom he meets on a train, into a criss-cross murder plot. (See page 8.)

### THE BIG HEAT
dir Fritz Lang, 1953
Based on the 1953 novel by William P. McGivern, this sees honest cop Glenn Ford investigating a colleague's suicide though told by superiors to back off. His determination increases when his wife is killed in a gangster hit meant for him. Deducing senior cops are in the pay of gangsters, Ford fights and defeats the corruption.

*The main thing is to have the money. I've been rich and I've been poor.*
*"Believe me, rich is better."*
The Big Heat (1953)

### SUDDENLY
dir Lewis Allen, 1954

A gang led by brutal, sadistic Frank Sinatra take over the home of James Gleason and family, imprisoning there also local cop Sterling Hayden, as a preliminary to making an assassination attempt on the US President. In the end it is down to Hayden to thwart the plot.

### KILLER'S KISS
dir Stanley Kubrick, 1955

Nightclub dancer Irene Kane and boxer Jamie Smith are in love, and plan to escape the city together. However, Kane's boss Frank Silvera wants Kane for himself, and kidnaps her to a warehouse where he sets a trap for Smith.

### THE PHENIX CITY STORY
dir Phil Karlson, 1955

Thugs employed by crime boss Edward Andrews murder district attorney John McIntire, and McIntire's crusading lawyer son Richard Kiley goes on the offensive against not just Andrews but all the corruption of "America's Wickedest City". Based on real events, and made even as some of the related trials were still running.

### TOUCH OF EVIL
dir Orson Welles, 1958

Based on the novel *Badge of Evil* (1956) by Whit Masterson. A bigwig is murdered on the Mexican border by a car bomb. The investigation sets Mexican cop Charlton Heston against irremediably corrupt US cop Orson Welles, who wants to fake evidence framing a young Mexican. Revolted, Heston tries to expose Welles, who retaliates with violence, kidnap and doublecross, trying to exploit Heston's love for his new wife Janet Leigh.

*"That's life. Whichever way you turn, Fate sticks out a foot to trip you."*
Detour (1945)

## VERTIGO
### dir Alfred Hitchcock, 1958

Based on the novel *D'Entre les Morts* (1956) by Pierre Boileau and Thomas Narcejac. Ex-cop James Stewart is hired as a P.I. to follow a wife, Kim Novak, who he's told has been suffering strange spells during which she seems possessed by the soul of a woman who suicided years ago. Stewart and Novak fall in love, but she seemingly commits suicide by throwing herself from a bell tower. Some while later, recuperating from his consequent breakdown, Stewart sees in the street a woman who's the double of his dead love, although with brown hair, not blonde. As the two become increasingly involved, the original seedy plot starts unravelling.

## CAPE FEAR
### dir J. Lee Thompson, 1962

Based on *The Executioners* (1958) by John D. MacDonald. Violent released convict Robert Mitchum terrorizes the family of lawyer Gregory Peck. Peck appeals to the police, but Mitchum is careful to keep his campaign of fear within the letter of the law. What becomes clear is that Peck, likewise, is really no more than a letter-of-the-law upstanding citizen. At last Peck resorts to straightforward violence, setting a trap for Mitchum in a remote spot.

The unnecessary 1991 remake, dir Martin Scorsese, adds nothing save enhanced violence and gloss.

## THE MANCHURIAN CANDIDATE
### dir John Frankenheimer, 1962

Based on the 1959 novel by Richard Condon. Korean war hero Laurence Harvey is a troubled man, not least because of buffoonish McCarthyish Senator stepfather James Gregory and scheming social-climber mother Angela Lansbury (a bravura performance). But there's worse. Old army colleague Frank Sinatra has dreams indicating Harvey's supposed heroism is a fiction. It emerges Harvey's patrol were seized and brainwashed/hypnotized in Korea to give them false memories, and that Harvey himself has been programmed to kill. Lansbury and Gregory are Fifth Columnists intent on securing the US Presidency. Despite its highly implausible premise, a surprisingly powerful movie.

# JAMES M. CAIN AND THE MOVIES

James Mallahan Cain was born in Annapolis in 1892 and as a child wanted to be an opera singer. Instead he entered journalism. The siren call of the movies took him to California in 1931. His novels include *The Postman Always Ring Twice* (1934), *Double Indemnity* (1936 serial; book publication 1944), *Serenade* (1937), *Mildred Pierce* (1941), *Love's Lonely Counterfeit* (1942), *Past All Dishonor* (1946), *The Butterfly* (1947), *The Moth* (1948), *Sinful Woman* (1948), *Jealous Woman* (1951), *The Root of His Evil* (1952; vt *The Modern Cinderella*), *Galatea* (1953), *Mignon* (1962), *The Magician's Wife* (1965), *Rainbow's End* (1975) and *The Institute* (1976). Short fiction of note included "The Baby in the Icebox" (1933), "Career in C Major" (1938; vt "*Two Can Sing*") and "*The Embezzler*" (1940). In 1970 he was named a Grand Master by the Mystery Writers of America. He died in University Park, Maryland, in 1977.

### THE BABY IN THE ICEBOX

Filmed as *She Made Her Bed* (1934), dir Ralph Murphy, scr Casey Robinson. Sally Eilers loathes carnival-owner husband Robert Armstrong and loves Richard Arlen. An escaped tiger threatens Eilers's baby. In fighting to save the child, Armstrong is killed. A fire breaks out, and in desperation Eilers stuffs the baby into the icebox. All ends happily. No masterpiece.

### TWO CAN SING

First filmed in 1939 as *Wife, Husband and Friend*, dir Gregory Ratoff, scr Nunnally Johnson. Loretta Young and Warner Baxter are singers who believe they are potential stars, and humiliatingly discover they're not.

This screwball comedy was remade in 1949 as *Everybody Does It*, dir Edmund Goulding, scr again Nunnally Johnson, who also produced. Here builder Paul Douglas and snooty wife Celeste Holm both think she has the makings of an opera star before glamorous diva Linda Darnell, taking a shine to Douglas, finds he's the one with the good singing voice.

## THE POSTMAN ALWAYS RINGS TWICE

This has been filmed several times. First came the French movie *Le Dernier Tournant* (1939), dir Pierre Chenal with a bevy of scripters. Drifter Fernand Gravey and luscious Corinne Luchaire fall in lust, and scheme to dispose of Luchaire's husband Michel Simon.

The second version was the Italian movie *Ossessione* (1942), dir Luchino Visconti, again with a passel of scripters (and with Cain's novel uncredited). Massimo Girotti is the drifter, Clara Calamai the *femme fatale*, and Juan De Landa her unwanted husband.

The third and most famous screen adaptation was *The Postman Always Rings Twice* (1946), dir Tay Garnett, scr Harry Ruskin and Niven Busch. John Garfield and Lana Turner are the two avaricious adulterers, Cecil Kellaway the husband. (See page 46.)

Bob Rafelson remade the 1946 movie in 1981 under the same title, scr David Mamet. Jack Nicholson and Jessica Lange are the couple, John Colicos the husband. For once the increased sexual content common in modern *noir* remakes is fully justified.

Filmed in black-and-white as if to stress its *noir* pedigree, the Hungarian movie *Szenvedély* (1998), dir György Fehér, has János Derzsi as the drifter, Ildikó Bánsági as the wife and Djoko Rosic as the husband.

As with Visconti's much earlier version, Cain's novel is uncredited in the 2004 Malaysian adaptation *Buai Laju-Laju* (vt *Swing My Swing High, My Darling*), dir U-Wai Haji Saari. Eman Manan is the drifter, Betty Banafe the wife, and Khalid Salleh the husband.

### THE ROOT OF HIS EVIL

This novel was written in various forms long before it saw publication in 1952. Thus, confusingly, the first movie adaptation, based on a version called "The Modern Cinderella", considerably predates the novel. This movie was *When Tomorrow Comes* (1939), dir John M. Stahl, scr Dwight Taylor. Charles Boyer is unhappily married, and runs off with waitress Irene Dunne for a torrid weekend on Long Island.

The first remake, *Interlude* (1957), dir Douglas Sirk, scr Daniel Fuchs and Franklin Coen, shifts the story to Europe, where visiting American June Allyson falls in love with conductor Rossano Brazzi.

The 1957 movie was remade, this time set in London, as *Interlude* (1968), dir Kevin Billington, scr Lee Langley and Hugh Leonard. Barbara Ferris and Oskar Werner are the lovers.

### THE EMBEZZLER

Filmed as *Money and the Woman* (1940), dir William Howard, scr Robert R. Presnell. Bank teller Roger Pryor has been embezzling funds for years. Visiting bank VP Jeffrey Lynn discovers this, but delays taking action for the sake of Pryor's wife Brenda Marshall, Lynn and Marshall having taken a fancy to each other. But then it emerges that Pryor has been two-timing her with Lee Patrick . . .

### DOUBLE INDEMNITY

The first movie version, *Double Indemnity* (1944), is one of the great classics of *noir*. Barbara Stanwyck produces a memorable performance as the siren who lures amoral insurance salesman Fred MacMurray into a plot to murder her husband. (See page 44.)

This was remade in 1973 with the same title as a TV movie, dir Jack Smight, script adapted from the Raymond Chandler/Billy Wilder original by Steven Bochco. Richard Crenna and Samantha Eggar are the two scheming lovers, Lee J. Cobb the wily old insurance investigator who smells a rat.

## MILDRED PIERCE

Joan Crawford stars as a waitress who's risen by struggle to become a restaurant-chain owner in *Mildred Pierce* (1945), dir Michael Curtiz, scr Ranald MacDougall. But all goes for nothing as she and spiteful daughter Ann Blyth compete for the affections of Zachary Scott, from whose murder the tale is told in flashback. Crawford took the Oscar for her part.

## LOVE'S LONELY COUNTERFEIT

Filmed as *Slightly Scarlet* (1955), dir Allan Dwan, scr Robert Blees, an early example of *noir* in SuperScope Technicolor. Low-level gangster John Payne is instructed to infiltrate the election campaign of a reformist mayoral candidate, but falls for secretary Rhonda Fleming and switches allegiance. Fleming's kleptomaniac *femme fatale* sister Arlene Dahl complicates matters.

## SERENADE

With all its homosexual parts expunged, this was filmed in 1956, dir Anthony Mann, scr Derek N. Twist. Humble vineyard worker Mario Lanza is turned into opera star by wealthy lover Joan Fontaine. When she dumps him just before his big audition, he flees in grief to Mexico, where he and Sarita Montiel fall in love. But then Fontaine reappears on the scene . . .

## BUTTERFLY

A minor novel made into a very minor movie, *Butterfly* (1982), dir Matt Cimber, scr Cimber and John Goff. Pia Zadora has trouble fighting off the unwelcome attentions of her father, Stacy Keach.

## ENCHANTED ISLE

This posthumous (1985) novella was filmed in 1995 as *Girl in the Cadillac*, dir Lucas Platt, scr John Warren. Teenage runaway Erika Eleniak falls in with William McNamara, who plots a heist with Michael Lerner and Bud Cort. The heist successful, Eleniak and McNamara make off with the loot, the other two in hot pursuit.

# A LIBRARY OF NEO-*NOIR*

There was no real start-date for the neo-*noir* period, for the very simple reason that the making of *noir* movies never entirely ceased after the Golden Age. However, there was a definite upturn of interest in the style from about the early 1970s onward, with movies like *Klute* (1971) and *Chinatown* (1974) paving the way. The movies briefly described in the next few pages together offer a cross-section of the continuing "neo" phase of the style.

### KLUTE
dir Alan J. Pakula, 1971

Small-town cop John Klute (Donald Sutherland) comes to the big city to investigate the disappearance of an acquaintance, his only lead being that his quarry may have been a client of prostitute Jane Fonda (in an Oscar-winning performance). The relentlessly impassive Sutherland (also Oscar-worthy) attempts to fathom the mystery of the equally alienated Fonda.

### CHINATOWN
dir Roman Polanski, 1974

In 1937 seedy LA private eye Jack Nicholson is duped into a plot to discredit public official Darrell Zwerling, who opposes construction of a new reservoir, photographing him with a young girl. Zwerling's vengeful wife Faye Dunaway, daughter of magnate John Huston, hires Nicholson when her husband is murdered. Pursuing the case, he unearths a corrupt scheme of huge proportions masterminded by Huston, also that the girl who seduced Zwerling is Huston's granddaughter through forced incestuous liaison with Dunaway.

### TAXI DRIVER
dir Martin Scorsese, 1976

Vietnam vet Robert De Niro now works as a taxi driver in New York, a city he loathes and despises. A gun freak, he concludes his mission is to rid the city of its "scum". In the finale, he guns down some of them and becomes a media hero. A movie outstanding for its portrayal of the seedy misery and squalor underpinning New York's glitz.

### BODY HEAT
dir Lawrence Kasdan, 1981

*Femme fatale* Kathleen Turner traps unscrupulous lawyer William Hurt in a web of sex until he is an all too willing colleague in her plot to rid herself of unwanted husband Richard Crenna and collect the insurance money. But there is much doublecrossing to come between the partners in crime.

### AGAINST ALL ODDS
dir Taylor Hackford, 1984

A much elaborated remake of *Out of the Past* (1947; see page 46). Injured football star Jeff Bridges is hired by petty LA gangster James Woods to find Woods's girlfriend Rachel Ward, who has run off to Mexico with a stack of Woods's money. Once she's found, the two fall in love. But she kills a man and flees back to Woods. Returning to LA in pursuit, Bridges faces large-scale corruption in high places.

### BLACK WIDOW
dir Bob Rafelson, 1987

Psychopathic *femme fatale* Theresa Russell has made a fortune from marrying wealthy men and then murdering them. At last loner fed Debra Winger spots the pattern and is on her trail. As the cat-and-mouse game proceeds, it becomes clear that the supposed mouse is really the cat; Winger's emotions become something akin to romantic love for Russell, leading one to wonder if she will be the Black Widow's next victim.

This is unrelated to a classic-era *noir* worth watching: *Black Widow* (1954), dir Nunnally Johnson, with a cast including George Raft, Ginger Rogers and Gene Tierney.

### SOMEONE TO WATCH OVER ME
dir Ridley Scott, 1987

Perhaps the most stylish of all neo-*noirs*, taking a standard *noir* plot – married cop Tom Berenger is assigned to protect murder witness and possible *femme fatale* Mimi Rogers, and the two breach the social barriers to fall in love – and making out of it something that is often moving and always aesthetically striking.

### THE GRIFTERS
dir Stephen Frears, 1990

Based on the 1963 novel by Jim Thompson. Anjelica Huston, her son John Cusack and his part-time hooker girlfriend Annette Beming con their way around the country, though never really hitting the big time. Despite events aplenty, the real plot of this movie lies in its subtext: Cusack's confused sexuality regarding the two women in his life, exacerbated by an obvious sexual component in Huston's supposedly maternal protectiveness.

### BASIC INSTINCT
dir Paul Verhoeven, 1992

Jaded, vile cop Michael Douglas becomes obsessed with lesbian serial killer and *femme fatale* Sharon Stone; she thrills adolescent males everywhere by flashing her pudenda at the camera; she and Douglas spend protracted periods balling. The "basic instinct" of the title is that lesbians just hate men and want to kill them all with icepicks; do Verhoeven and scripter Joe Eszterhas just hate women or are they frightened of them too?

### STORYVILLE
dir Mark Frost, 1992

Lawyer James Spader, scion of a hugely wealthy Southern family, is running for Congress against a racist bigot while still puzzling over his father's apparent suicide. His seemingly chance seduction by an alluring beauty (Charlotte Lewis) leads to murder and also to the unravelling of his father's homicide and the family history of moral and financial deception.

### CHINA MOON
dir John Bailey, 1994

Florida private eye Ed Harris is lured by *femme fatale* Madeleine Stowe into hiding the body after the murder of her fabulously wealthy abusive husband, and then of course is made the prime suspect.

### THE LAST SEDUCTION
dir John Dahl, 1994

The ultimate *femme fatale* movie. High-powered exec Linda Fiorentino, revolted when drug-dealing husband Bill Pullman hits her, flees with the proceeds of his latest big sale, eventually finding herself in the sleepy town of Beston. There she picks up local stud Peter Berg and a job; Bill Nunn, the P.I. whom Pullman sends after her, is summarily despatched. Berg, easily bamboozled and screwed senseless, is deceived into trying to murder Pullman. Fiorentino, Dahl and the movie were talked about in Oscar terms, but all were ineligible because *The Last Seduction* was made for cable channel HBO and premiered there before cinematic release.

### PULP FICTION
dir Quentin Tarantino, 1994

Two hit men – John Travolta and Samuel L. Jackson – go about their day-to-day business of perpetrating mayhem, wisecracking incessantly while doing so. This device allows Tarantino to offer a diversity of *noir* scenarios – a sort of review of the field. The movie is much admired for its narrative flair and its many strong performances.

### DEVIL IN A BLUE DRESS
dir Carl Franklin, 1995

Based on the 1990 novel by Walter Mosley. Denzel Washington, out of work in 1948 LA, is hired by Tom Sizemore to track down Jennifer Beals, missing mistress of a prominent politician: he is qualified to help because, being black, he can ask around for her in the black bars she frequents. The ubiquitous racism of 1940s LA is as much his foe as the doublecrossing by his supposed colleagues. In desperation he brings in friend Don Cheadle, a hood whose language of choice is bullets, to sort out the mess. Washington solves the case but loses his innocence.

### SE7EN
dir David Fincher, 1995

Psychopath Kevin Spacey is staging his murders according to a pattern reflecting the Seven Deadly Sins. It takes abrasive newcomer cop Brad Pitt and wily old cop Morgan Freeman a while to recognize this, but then the hunt is on. The trouble is that they – and Pitt's pregnant wife Gwyneth Paltrow – may be the hunted rather than the hunters.

### THINGS TO DO IN DENVER WHEN YOU'RE DEAD
dir Gary Fleder, 1995

Retired and honourable hood Andy Garcia is persuaded to do a "frightener" job for vile ex-boss Christopher Walken, but it goes wrong. Walken vengefully calls in super-hitman Steve Buscemi to kill off Garcia's team: Bill Nunn, William Forsythe, Christopher Lloyd, Treat Williams. Though Garcia has just fallen in love with Gabrielle Anwar, he tries to protect his team even at the cost of his own life.

### THE USUAL SUSPECTS
dir Bryan Singer, 1995

Told almost entirely in flashback as the cops interview survivor Kevin Spacey, this follows five small-time crooks who're brought together for a police line-up and decide to perform a heist together. After the heist, it gradually becomes evident to them that they're not independent agents but pawns in someone else's unknown game. Spacey won an Oscar for his portrayal of crippled, awkward crook Verbal; Christopher McQuarrie won another for his script.

### FARGO
dir Joel Coen, 1996

Failing car salesman William H. Macy sets up a plot to have his wife kidnapped by bumbling hoods Steve Buscemi and Peter Stormare for the ransom her wealthy father is bound to produce. But things go wrong after the kidnap and the hoods initiate a murder spree that brings heavily pregnant cop Frances McDormand (deservedly Oscar-winning) into the case.

### LOST HIGHWAY
dir David Lynch, 1997

Sax player Bill Pullman and wife Patricia Arquette receive videos seemingly shot by a nocturnal visitor to their home. When Arquette is murdered, Pullman is convicted, but one night he is inexplicably replaced on Death Row by a much confused Balthazar Getty, who has of course to be released. Soon he is inveigled into an affair with gangster's moll and likely *femme fatale* Arquette, now going under a different name. Thereafter this bizarre *noir* is unsynopsizable.

### L.A. CONFIDENTIAL
dir Curtis Hanson, 1997

Based on the 1990 novel by James Ellroy, this enormously complicated movie has muckraking journalist Danny DeVito as guide to a complex tale involving three cops – straight arrow Guy Pearce, tough bull Russell Crowe and over-slick Kevin Spacey – as they investigate a restaurant massacre against a backdrop of racism, corruption, police brutality and ruthlessness.

### EYE OF THE BEHOLDER
dir Stephan Elliott, 1998

Based loosely on the 1980 novel by Mark Behm – filmed earlier by Claude Miller as *Mortelle Randonnée* (1983; vt *Deadly Circuit*, vt *Deadly Run*). Undercover agent Ewan McGregor becomes obsessed with serial killer Ashley Judd, tracking her and sometimes protecting her as she murders far and wide, seeing in her an echo of his missing daughter. A wonderful portrait of obsession.

### JACKIE BROWN
dir Quentin Tarantino, 1998

Based on the novel *Rum Punch* (1992) by Elmore Leonard. Airline stewardess Pam Grier is caught by the feds with cash and drugs and persuaded to act as mole in the organization of murderous gunrunner Samuel L. Jackson. Helped by bail bondsman Robert Forster, she successfully plays crooks and feds against each other. Grier's is a standout among a host of exceptional performances.

### MEMENTO
dir Christopher Nolan, 2000

Insurance investigator Guy Pearce suffered brain damage attempting to prevent the murder of his wife. Now, despite short-term memory loss, he is trying to identify her killer, his only tools being polaroids he has taken, annotating their backs, and tattoos he has commissioned on his body – his mementoes. Aid is offered by attractive Carrie-Anne Moss and garrulous Joe Pantoliano, but can they be trusted? The tale is told in the form of flashbacks, each progressively further in the past than the last – effectively, we see events in reverse order. This *tour de force* was not so much released as leaked onto the market, and defied the marketers by outperforming many "blockbusters".

### REINDEER GAMES
(vt *Deception*)
dir John Frankenheimer, 2000

Frankenheimer returns to his roots with this *noir* tale of multiple doublecross, complete with a snaky *femme fatale*. Convict Ben Affleck sees his cellmate murdered days before their release, and decides to adopt his identity to hook up with the dead man's scrummy penpal girlfriend Charlize Theron. Within minutes of meeting they're in bed. Then her psychopathic brother Gary Sinise appears on the scene, and Affleck must aid a casino heist or die. Doublecross piles upon doublecross . . .

### MULHOLLAND DRIVE
dir David Lynch, 2001

Naive Naomi Watts arrives in Hollywood in search of stardom. She finds amnesic *femme fatale* Laura Elena Harring, who clearly needs to be taken under Watts's wing. The pair try to solve the mystery of who Harring is and become emotionally and sexually entangled. The trail leads to some sort of resolution – and murder – on Mulholland Drive. But is this what really happened? In a masterly *volte face*, various oddities from earlier in the movie begin to make sense as we're introduced to the notion that we've seen the fantasy Watts created to protect herself from a sordid reality.

### LIBERTY STANDS STILL
dir Kari Skogland, 2002

Ex-covert-operations sniper Wesley Snipes, whose daughter has been murdered, pins down corrupt arms dealer Linda Fiorentino in a Manhattan park as public protest against increasingly pro-gun legislation enacted by bribed senators and congressmen. As the vigil draws on and the two converse by radio, it becomes evident the network of "influence" extends far and deep within the establishment.

### TOUGH LUCK
dir Gary Ellis, 2003

Hopeless grifter Norman Reedus is hired by carnival-owner Assante to kill Assante's much younger wife Dagmara Dominczyk. The two scheme to doublecross Assante, except that it's Reedus, the born loser, who's being doublecrossed. A while later he encounters Dominczyk again, and is fool enough to fall in with her plans when she outlines a far more major piece of "business" . . .

### COLLATERAL
dir Michael Mann, 2004

LA cabdriver Jamie Foxx picks up beautiful lawyer Jada Pinkett Smith from the airport, and they establish a sort of friendship on the way into town. His next fare, though, is hitman Tom Cruise, whose m.o. is in each new city to hold a cabdriver at gunpoint while carrying out his hits, then kill the cabbie, framing him for the murders. Tonight the final victim on Cruise's list is Pinkett Smith. Foxx turns in an Oscar-deserving performance (his Oscar that year was instead for his lead role in *Ray*), while Cruise offers surprisingly good support.

*"They've committed a murder and it's not like
taking a trolley ride together, where they can get off at
different stops. They're stuck with each other and
they've got to ride all the way to the end of the line, and
it's a one-way trip and the last stop is
the cemetery."*
Double Indemnity (1944)

# CORNELL WOOLRICH AND THE MOVIES

Born in New York in 1903, Cornell George Hopley-Woolrich (aka William Irish and George Hopley) had a life shrouded in as much mystery as any of his fictions.

Woolrich was an inveterate fancifier, so nothing he said about himself can be trusted and much has been proven false. He was a loner, almost certainly because of unconfessed homosexuality; his fictions are full of loneliness, paranoia and fear. His crime novels were: *The Bride Wore Black* (1940), *The Black Curtain* (1941), *The Black Alibi* (1942), *The Black Angel* (1943), *The Black Path of Fear* (1944), *Rendezvous in Black* (1948), *Savage Bride* (1950), *Hotel Room* (1958), *Death is My Dancing Partner* (1959) and *The Doom Stone* (1960), all as by Cornell Woolrich; *Night Has a Thousand Eyes* (1945), *Fright* (1950), both as by George Hopley; *Phantom Lady* (1942), *Deadline at Dawn* (1944), *Waltz into Darkness* (1947), *I Married a Dead Man* (1948) and *Bluebeard's Seventh Wife* (1952), all as by William Irish. There are also various volumes of short stories. He died in New York in 1968.

Over 60 movies have been made based on Woolrich's works. An exact count is probably impossible: while there are known instances of movies based on specific works by Woolrich which have not credited him, it's anyone's guess as to how many others there are of this ilk. The following listing is thus selective.

### THE BLACK CURTAIN

Filmed in 1942 as *Street of Chance*, dir Jack Hively, scr Garrett Fort. Burgess Meredith wakes up with no clue as to how he got where he is except the initials "D.N." on his hat and cigarette case. He traces wife Louise Platt, who tells him he has been missing for over a year. During that time, did he become engaged to *femme fatale* Claire Trevor, and did he commit murder?

## THE BLACK ALIBI

Filmed as *The Leopard Man* (1943), scr Ardel Wray and starring Dennis O'Keefe, this was one of the three movies Jacques Tourneur directed at the outset of producer Val Lewton's tenure as head of RKO's B-movie division. A town on the Mexican border is being terrorized. Is the culprit an escaped leopard or a far more dangerous, two-legged animal?

## PHANTOM LADY

Robert Siodmak directed *Phantom Lady* (1944), scr Bernard C. Schoenfeld. Alan Curtis is sentenced to die for murdering his wife, even though at the time of the killing he was attending a musical with an anonymous belle. Secretary Ella Raines races against the clock, using all her feminine wiles, to try to prove his innocence.

## BLACK ANGEL

In *Black Angel* (1946), dir Roy William Neill, scr Roy Chanslor, estranged wife Constance Dowling of alcoholic composer Dan Duryea is murdered, and John Phillips is convicted of the crime. With Phillips's wife June Vincent, Duryea explores the low life in search of the real killer.

A 1967 Japanese remake, *Yoru No Wana*, dir Sokichi Tomimoto, starred Akiya Manabe and Ayako Wakao as the husband and wife, Masahiko Naruse as the cop.

## THE BLACK PATH OF FEAR

This was filmed as *The Chase* (1946), dir Arthur Ripley, scr Philip Yordan. Robert Cummings is chauffeur to shady businessman Steve Cochran, and become entangled with Cochran's wife Michele Morgan. The lovers plan to flee to Havana, but Cummings has an ominous dream this will lead to doom.

### DEADLINE AT DAWN

Harold Clurman directed and Clifford Odets scripted *Deadline at Dawn* (1946). Sailor on shore-leave Bill Williams spent time while drunk with *femme fatale* Lola Lane, though he can remember nothing of what happened, and now she's been murdered. With the help of Susan Hayward he must try to prove his innocence and find the killer before his leave is up. This was remade in Turkey by Memduh Ün as *Bire on Vardi* (1963).

### NIGHTMARE

The 1941 story "And So to Death" (better known by its vt "Nightmare") was first filmed by Maxwell Shane as *Fear in the Night* (1947). De Forest Kelley dreams he murders a man in a mirrored room, and next day finds evidence this might not have been a dream. Cop brother-in-law Paul Kelly initially believes it was a dream, then suspects Kelley, finally deduces Kelley was hypnotized.

Director Maxwell Shane had a second stab at this with the much better *Nightmare* (1956). Kevin McCarthy was the "dreamer" and Edward G. Robinson the cop.

### I WOULDN'T BE IN YOUR SHOES

This 1938 short story was filmed in 1948, dir William Nigh, scr Steve Fisher. Don Castle is convicted of murder, and wife Elyse Knox, with the help of kindly cop Regis Toomey, tries to clear his name.

### NIGHT HAS A THOUSAND EYES

John Farrow directed and Barre Lyndon and Jonathan Latimer scripted this paranormal *noir* in 1948. Edward G. Robinson meets engaged couple Gail Russell and John Lund and tells them he used to be a fake psychic until becoming gifted with genuine precognitive powers. He hid himself away when he learned his fiancée was going to die in childbirth; instead she married Russell's father and indeed died giving birth to Russell. Now, Robinson says, Russell herself is in deadly danger . . .

## THE BOY CRIED MURDER

Based on the 1947 story "The Boy Cried Murder", *The Window* (1949) was dir Ted Tetzlaff and scr Mel Dinelli. One night Bobby Driscoll, a habitual liar, sees a murder. No one will believe his story, and the murderers have him marked as their next victim. This clearly prefigures *Rear Window* (1954).

The movie was remade in 1966 as a UK/West German/Yugoslavian coproduction, *The Boy Cried Murder*, dir George P. Breakston, scr Robin Estridge. Fraser MacIntosh was the boy who'd lied too often before.

In 1984 the story was very loosely adapted as *Cloak & Dagger*, dir Richard Franklin. Here the small boy (Henry Thomas) is aided in his flight from the baddies by his favourite comic-book character, Jack Flack (Dabney Coleman), whose status in reality is pleasantly ambiguous.

## I MARRIED A DEAD MAN

First filmed in 1950 as *No Man of Her Own*, dir Mitchell Leisen, scr Sally Benson and Catherine Turney. Barbara Stanwyck, unmarried and pregnant, survives a train crash and takes on the identity of a young bride killed with her husband in the accident. She is accepted by the dead man's wealthy family, but then lover Lyle Bettger finds her and starts blackmailing her.

This was remade in France as *J'ai Épousé une Ombre* (1983; vt *I Married a Dead Man*, vt *I Married a Shadow*), dir Robin Davis, scr Patrick Laurent. Nathalie Baye was the impostor, Richard Bohringer the blackmailer, in what is the only attempt to translate Woolrich to the vineyards of Bordeaux.

A further adaptation, this time as fluffy comedy, was *Mrs. Winterbourne* (1996), dir Richard Benjamin, scr Phoef Sutton and Lisa-Maria Radano. Ricki Lake is the false bride, Loren Dean the unwanted boyfriend.

Yet another remake, this time with Woolrich uncredited, was the

TV movie *She's No Angel* (2005), dir/scr Rachel Feldman. Tracey Gold is a rape victim who thinks she's found security when taken in by vintners Kevin Dobson and Dee Wallace-Stone.

### REAR WINDOW

Dir Alfred Hitchcock, scr John Michael Hayes based on the story "It Had to Be Murder" (1942), *Rear Window* (1954) is among the most famous suspense movies. Trapped in his apartment with a broken leg, James Stewart spies on his neighbours and believes he sees evidence that Raymond Burr has murdered his wife. He convinces girlfriend Grace Kelly and day-nurse Thelma Ritter, but no one else. Then Burr becomes aware he's being spied upon . . .

A TV-movie remake came in 1998, dir Jeff Bleckner, scr Eric Overmyer and Larry Gross, with Christopher Reeve and Daryl Hannah in the central roles. Reeve was wheelchair-bound in real life, so well equipped to give a knowledgeable performance.

### THE BRIDE WORE BLACK

Filmed by François Truffaut, *La Mariée Était en Noir* (1967; vt *The Bride Wore Black*). Jeanne Moreau is widowed within moments of her marriage, her groom shot down on the church steps, and sets out to bump off those responsible one by one.

### WALTZ INTO DARKNESS

Truffaut returned to Woolrich for his 1969 movie *La Sirène du Mississippi* (vt *Mississippi Mermaid*). Réunion-based cigarette manufacturer Jean-Paul Belmondo advertises for a wife and is lucky enough to get *femme fatale* Catherine Deneuve. Even as the dreadful truths begin to appear about her real nature, he thinks it's worth it.

The remake was the 2001 US/French coproduction *Original Sin* (vt *Péché Originel*), dir and scr Michael Cristofer. Antonio Banderas is a Cuban coffee trader in early-20th-century Cuba, Angelina Jolie the con-artist bride.

*"My, my, my! Such a lot of guns around town and so few brains!"*
The Big Sleep (1946)

*"Besides, what does a dame like you want with a guy like me?"*
Sorry, Wrong Number (1948)

*"It's funny, but practically all the people I know were
strangers when I met them."*
The Blue Dahlia (1946)

*"Stop making noises like a husband."*
Detour (1945)

*"You know, a dame with a rod is like a guy with
a knitting needle."*
Out of the Past (1947)

*"Listen, any girl that waits two hours in the rain for
a guy is gonna give him a dirty look."*
Scarlet Street (1945)

*"You shouldn't keep souvenirs of a killing.
You shouldn't have been that sentimental."*
Vertigo (1958)

*"When an alibi is full of bourbon, sir, it can't stand up."*
Strangers on a Train (1951)

*"Funny, how gentle people get with you once you're dead."*
Sunset Boulevard (1950)

*"A boy's best friend is his mother."*
Psycho (1960)

# A LIBRARY OF INTERNATIONAL *NOIR*

Although *film noir* is "the American Style", other countries have produced *noirs* aplenty, some in imitation of the US breed, some in their own wholly original style. Of particular note are the French *noirs*, which are many and often distinguished, while the UK is another country to have produced a good share of fine *noir* movies.

### GASLIGHT
dir Thorold Dickinson, 1940, UK

The first of two movies, both good but this one excellent, based on the 1938 play *Gas Light* (vt *Angel Street*) by Patrick Hamilton. Wealthy but naive Diana Wynyard marries gold-digger Anton Walbrook, who plots to have her declared insane so he can control her money. Scotland Yard detective Frank Pettingell becomes suspicious – and attracted to Wynyard.

The unnecessary and undesirably more lavish 1944 US remake was dir George Cukor and starred Charles Boyer and Ingrid Bergman. To protect their investment, MGM ordered all copies of the earlier movie destroyed. Luckily this act of cultural terrorism was not entirely successful.

### QUAI DES ORFÈVRES
(vt *Jenny Lamour*)
dir Henri-Georges Clouzot, 1947, France

On the verge of retirement, police inspector Louis Jouvet takes on one last case, the murder of the lover of singer Suzy Delair, whose marriage is on the skids. The body is discovered by Delair's husband Bernard Blier, who is slowly persuaded his wife must be guilty. But . . .

Almost more important than the plot is the Hitchcockian treatment. The movie was at the time regarded in the Anglo-Saxon world as very shocking because of its forthright treatment of sex.

### THE THIRD MAN
dir Carol Reed, 1949, UK

Scr Graham Greene, this movie — thanks to designer Vincent Korda and cinematographer Robert Krasker — reads like the very best of Hitchcock or Welles (who in fact acts in it, and who contributed material to the script). Amid the ruins of post-war Vienna, US visitor Joseph Cotten seeks the murderer of his friend Harry Lime (Orson Welles), only to find Lime arranged his own "death" and is still alive as a base criminal.

### LE SALAIRE DE LA PEUR
(vt *The Wages of Fear*)
dir Henri-Georges Clouzot, 1953, France/Italy

Four expats in a South American banana republic (Yves Montand, Charles Vanel, Peter Van Eyck and Folco Lulli) are hired to drive two truckloads of nitroglycerine over dangerous roads to an American oilfield. As the stresses mount on them, rather than develop cozy Hollywood-style fraternal loyalties to each other, they become ever more prepared to sacrifice each other in their individual pursuit of greed.

The movie was badly remade by William Friedkin as *Sorcerer* (1977; vt *The Wages of Fear*).

### LES DIABOLIQUES
(vt *Diabolique*, vt *The Fiends*)
dir Henri-Georges Clouzot, 1964, France

Based on the 1954 novel *Celle qui n'Était Plus* (vt *The Woman Who Was*) by Pierre Boileau and Thomas Narcejac; Clouzot apparently beat Alfred Hitchcock by just a few hours in the race to buy the movie rights. Brutal private-school headmaster Paul Meurisse married sickly wife Véra Clouzot only for her money, and is eager that she die from her long-threatened heart failure. Spurred on by Meurisse's mistress Simone Signoret, Clouzot decides to be the worm that turns, and the two women mount a byzantine scheme to murder him while giving themselves a watertight alibi.

The 1996 Hollywood remake, starring Isabelle Adjani, Chazz Palminteri, Kathy Bates and Sharon Stone, is partially saved by Adjani's performance as the vulnerable wife and Bates's as the cop. A better, earlier US remake was *Reflections of Murder* (1974) dir John Badham.

### TOUCHEZ PAS AU GRISBI
(vt *Grisbi*, vt *Honour Among Thieves*, vt *Paris Underground*)
dir Jacques Becker, 1954, France/Italy

The progenitor of a whole string of French crime movies. Gangster Jean Gabin plans to retire from the fray after one last heist, but rival gangster Lino Ventura – who has heard about the robbery through their shared mistress Jeanne Moreau – kidnaps Gabin's comrade-in-crime René Dary and demands the proceeds of the heist as ransom.

### BOB LE FLAMBEUR
(vt *Bob the Gambler*)
dir Jean-Pierre Melville, 1955, France

In 1935 Paris, the very gentlemanly, almost chivalric gambler Bob (Roger Duchesne) decides to organize a heist at the casino where he habitually gambles. His young friends Daniel Cauchy and Isabelle Corey are to perform the robbery while Bob himself gambles there; but then things go wrong and Cauchy is killed. Meanwhile Bob's old adversary and friend, the police inspector Guy Decomble, having heard of the planned heist, descends. The irony is that Bob, on a winning streak, has forgotten to play his part in the theft ... but has won the precise sum the robbery was supposed to net.

### DU RIFIFI CHEZ LES HOMMES
(vt *Rififi*)
dir Jules Dassin, 1955, France

Jewel thieves Robert Manuel, Carl Mohner, director Dassin himself (as Perlo Vita) and their mortally ill mastermind, Jean

Servais, perform a major jewellery heist only to find a rival gang, led by Marcel Lupovici, moving in to seize the spoils. Dassin was an American who, because of the McCarthy witch-hunts, moved to work in Europe and there made a string of commercial and critical successes, including *Topkapi* (1964).

### THE LADYKILLERS
dir Alexander Mackendrick, 1955, UK

A rare example of a *noir* comedy. Thieves Alec Guinness, Peter Sellers, Cecil Parker, Herbert Lom and Danny Green descend upon the boardinghouse of kindly old lady Katy Johnson in the guise of a string quartet seeking rehearsal space. The plan is, rather, to rob a local bank, and in this they succeed. Their inability to ignore the social niceties in their dealings with the oblivious Johnson leads to an unravelling, and they turn murderously upon each other. A completely unnecessary but unexpectedly good remake was *The Ladykillers* (2004), dir Ethan and Joel Coen, starring Tom Hanks as the ringleader and a magnificent Irma P. Hall as the landlady.

### MAIGRET TEND UN PIÈGE
(vt *Maigret Lays a Trap*, vt *Maigret Sets a Trap*)
dir Jean Delannoy, 1957, France/Italy

Based on the 1955 novel by Georges Simenon. A serial killer stalks Paris, slaying women. Maigret (Jean Gabin, in the first of three appearances in the role) investigates, and picks up architect Jean Desailly as his suspect. However, while Desailly is in custody the killer strikes again . . . or does he? There are enough differences in the m.o. to make Maigret suspicious. This was remade as a French TV movie in 1996 with the same title, dir Juraj Herz.

### À BOUT DE SOUFFLE
(vt *Breathless*)
dir Jean-Luc Godard, 1959, France

Petty Marseilles criminal Jean-Paul Belmondo models himself on Humphrey Bogart. He senselessly guns down a cop and goes into hiding in Paris, where he is owed money by a mysterious paymaster. He shelters in the home of a young American, Jean Seberg, and they become lovers. At last, though, it is Seberg who helps the cops corner and kill him. The movie was remade poorly as *Breathless* (1983), dir Jim McBride, with Richard Gere and Valerie Kaprisky in the Belmondo/Seberg roles.

### PLEIN SOLEIL
(vt *Purple Noon*, vt *Blazing Sun*)
dir René Clément, 1960, France/Italy

Based on Patricia Highsmith's *The Talented Mr Ripley* (1955), this has Alain Delon as an icily psychopathic Ripley driven to murder by financial greed, by lust, and by the despicable behaviour of the playboy American (Maurice Ronet) he has been sent to "rescue" from a life of Mediterranean decadence; the lust is for Ronet's girlfriend Marie Laforest.

### SEANCE ON A WET AFTERNOON
dir Bryan Forbes, 1964, UK

Based on the 1961 novel by Mark McShane. Fake medium Kim Stanley has ever been in denial about the stillbirth of her son, and now claims him as her contact with the spirit world. To boost her reputation she persuades husband Richard Attenborough to kidnap a child and claim the ransom; she will then "psychically" guide the cops to the child. A distinctly creepy *noir* with a highly fantasticated affect born of Stanley's insanity.

The movie was remade in Japan as *Korei* (2000; vt *Séance*) dir Kiyoshi Kurosawa.

### KOROSHI NO RAKUIN
(vt *Branded to Kill*)
dir Seijun Suzuki, 1967, Japan

A near-neurotic hitman known as Number 3 Killer (Shishido Joe) becomes obsessed with a *femme fatale* (Annu Mari). When she commissions him for a hit, he bungles it. His unfaithful wife tries to kill him. And someone sets the more successful Number 1 Killer on his trail. The Nikkatsu Corporation, which released *Koroshi no Rakuin*, fired Susuki after doing so on the grounds that he was creating incomprehensible movies that lost money. The movie, which is complex and surrealist, has come to be regarded as a precursor of the work of the likes of David Lynch.

### LE SAMOURAÏ
(vt *The Samurai*)
dir Jean-Pierre Melville, 1967, France/Italy

Contract killer Alain Delon is instructed to kill witness Cathy Rosier even though she has sworn to keep silent. He has his own *bushido*-like code of honour, though, and faces a dilemma. Martin Scorsese's *Taxi Driver* (1976) is a near-homage to this movie, while Walter Hill's *The Driver* (1978) reads almost like a remake of it.

### LE BOUCHER
(vt *The Butcher*)
dir Claude Chabrol, 1969, France

In a small Périgord town, schoolmistress Stéphane Audran and ex-soldier, now butcher Jean Yanne fall in love. A brace of brutal sex murders terrorizes the community, and Audran realizes Yanne is the culprit. However, she keeps her secret until Yanne confronts her alone with his lethal butcher-knife.

### MILANO ODIA: LA POLIZIA NON PUÒ SPARARE
(vt *Almost Human*, vt *The Kidnap of Mary Lou*)
dir Umberto Lenzi, 1974, Italy

Extraordinarily violent *noir* melodrama in which amphetamine-addicted petty gangster Tomas Milian reacts with paranoia to accusations of cowardice in an abortive bank heist, going on a protracted kidnapping and killing spree in Milan, machine gun in hand. Pursuing him is dour cop Henry Silva.

### DER AMERIKANISCHE FREUND
(vt *L'Ami Américain*, vt *The American Friend*)
dir Wim Wenders, 1977, West Germany/France

Based on Patricia Highsmith's 1974 novel *Ripley's Game*. Ripley (Dennis Hopper) latches onto Hamburg picture restorer Bruno Ganz, who has an incurable blood disease. Ripley proposes Ganz to gangster Gérard Blain as candidate to be the amateur hitman Blain seeks: Ganz is dying, so what would he have to lose? Ganz makes the hit, but Blain withholds half the fee until he performs another . . . The movie is full of homages to American *noir*, from frequent Hitchcockian allusions to the casting in cameo roles of classic directors Nicholas Ray and Samuel Fuller.

### SÉRIE NOIRE
dir Alain Corneau, 1979, France

Based on Jim Thompson's novel *A Hell of a Woman* (1954), this sees door-to-door salesman Patrick Dewaere murder an old woman to steal cash from her. The title is an allusion to the famous pulp-fiction series whose name gave rise to the term "*film noir*". (See page 82.)

### DIE SENSUCHT DER VERONIKA VOSS
(vt *Veronika Voss*)
dir Rainer Werner Fassbinder, 1982, West Germany

It is 1955. Veronika Voss (Rosel Zech) was a movie star under the Reich and cannot face the reality that her light terminally waned when the Reich fell. Into her path stumbles alcoholic sports journalist Hilmar Thate, who becomes infatuated with her. After he sleeps with Veronika he begins, with his long-suffering girlfriend's assistance, to probe into the mystery of Voss's current situation, and finds she is in the clutches of a phony neurologist whose gang addicts rich "patients" to morphine and sleeping pills, leeches all their property from them, then engineers their suicides. Shot in black-and-white, the movie is almost a route-map of *noir*.

### POULET AU VINAIGRE
(vt *Cop au Vin*)
dir Claude Chabrol, 1984, France

Small-town postman Lucas Belvaux, aided by crippled mother Stéphane Audran, investigates the brutal murder of a local entrepreneur, but the solution eludes him until Inspecteur Lavardin (Jean Poiret) arrives on the scene. This was the first of two Inspecteur Lavardin movies Chabrol made, the other being called simply *Inspecteur Lavardin* (1986).

### SPOORLOOS
(vt *The Vanishing*)
dir George Sluizer, 1988, Netherlands/France

Based on Tim Krabbé's novel *Het Gouden Ei* (1984). Holidaying Dutch couple Gene Bervoets and Johanna Ter Steege stop at a gas station; Ter Steege goes to the ladies' room and never reappears. Three years later, abductor Bernard-Pierre Dannadieu contacts the tormented Bervoets by postcard with offers to reveal the woman's fate. A movie of colossal psychological impact, *Spoorloos* was internationally successful, and Sluizer was brought to Hollywood to direct a remake, *The Vanishing* (1993), starring Kiefer Sutherland and Jeff Bridges. Unfortunately, the remake was Hollywoodized to mediocrity.

### KISS OR KILL
dir Bill Bennett, 1997, Australia

A victim dies on scam artists Frances O'Connor and Matt Day, and they find in his possessions a child-porn video featuring celebrity Barry Langrishe. As the grifters flee Langrishe and the cops, they leave a trail of bodies seemingly slain by a sleepwalking O'Connor. But nothing's that simple in this atmospheric road-movie *noir*.

### DIRTY PRETTY THINGS
dir Stephen Frears, 2002, UK

The horrific underbelly of modern UK society. Audrey Tautou, a Turk wishing she could join her sister in New York, and Chiwetel Ejiofor, a Nigerian doctor driven from his homeland by corrupt government officials, struggle to survive in modern London. Their illegal-immigrant status leaves them open to the most inhumane exploitation from all sides. But at the last they are able to turn the tables on sinister illegal-organ trader Sergi López and escape with their essential integrity intact. Sterling support performances from Benedict Wong and Sophie Okonedo.

Ann Miller: "*She can't be all bad. No one is.*"
Jeff Bailey: "*Well, she comes the closest.*"
Out of the Past (1947)

# JIM THOMPSON AND THE MOVIES

James Meyers Thompson was born in Anadarko, Oklahoma, in 1906. He had a mixed career, including working for the Works Projects Administration's Federal Writers' Project, before turning to fiction, publishing his first novel, *Now and on Earth*, in 1942. A string of novels followed through the 1940s, the 1950s and the first half of the 1960s; thereafter his output diminished. Also during the 1950s and the first half of the 1960s he did some Hollywood work, including scripting *Paths of Glory* (1957) and writing additional dialogue for *The Killing* (1956). Throughout his career, he was hindered by alcoholism and consequent cash shortages; he was also a victim of the McCarthy witch-hunts. Jim Thompson died in 1977 in Hollywood.

His novels include *Heed the Thunder* (1946), *Nothing More than Murder* (1949), *Cropper's Cabin* (1952), *The Killer Inside Me* (1952), *The Alcoholics* (1953), *Bad Boy* (1953), *The Criminal* (1953), *Recoil* (1953), *Savage Night* (1953), *A Swell-Looking Babe* (1954), *The Golden Gizmo* (1954), *A Hell of a Woman* (1954), *The Nothing Man* (1954), *Roughneck* (1954), *After Dark, My Sweet* (1954), *The Kill-Off* (1957), *Wild Town* (1957), *The Getaway* (1959), *The Transgressors* (1961), *The Grifters* (1963), *Pop. 1280* (1964), *Texas by the Tail* (1965), *Child of Rage* (1972), *King Blood* (1973) and *The Rip-Off* (1987), as well as the 1967 novelization of the TV series *Ironside*. "This World, Then the Fireworks" first appeared in 1988 in *Fireworks: The Lost Writings*.

## THE GETAWAY

First filmed in 1972 by Sam Peckinpah, scr Walter Hill. Steve McQueen does a heist for the mob that goes awry. The mob abduct wife Ali MacGraw as hostage for the money he hasn't got. Only through violence can he get her and the money, and escape to Mexico.

The remake came in 1994, dir Roger Donaldson, scr Amy Jones based on Walter Hill's original. Alex Baldwin is the Steve McQueen figure, released from jail through wife Kim Basinger prostituting herself to shady politician James Woods.

### THE KILLER INSIDE ME

Filmed by Burt Kennedy, scr Edward Mann and Robert Chamblee, *The Killer Inside Me* (1976) stars Stacy Keach as a small-town deputy sheriff who hides his murderous psychopathy behind a wisecracking, everybody's-friend mask. The movie succeeds in conveying some of the power of the remarkable novel.

### A HELL OF A WOMAN

Filmed in France as *Série Noir* (1979), dir Alain Corneau, who coscripted with Georges Perec. Patrick Dewaere, overacting, is a slow-witted, married door-to-door salesman seduced by pretty young Marie Trintignant into a scheme to murder her nasty aunt. Soon he is in the clutches of blackmailer Bernard Blier.

### POP. 1280

The basis for the French movie *Coup de Torchon* (1981; vt *Clean Slate*), dir Bertrand Tavernier, who coscripted with Jean Aurenche. In a colony in West Africa, French cop Philippe Noiret is inspired by legally killing a couple of pimps to start murdering white racists and eventually others, including wife Stéphane Audran and mistress Isabelle Huppert.

## THE KILL-OFF

Maggie Greenwald filmed and scripted this under its original title in 1989. In a small coastal resort, a community of disgusting characters is united in the urge to kill invalid Loretta Gross, whose malevolent gossip spreads their vilest secrets all over town.

## AFTER DARK, MY SWEET

James Foley directed and coscripted with Robert Redlin *After Dark, My Sweet* (1990). Bruce Dern and Rachel Ward recruit ex-boxer Jason Patric, who's on the run from a mental institution, to assist them in the kidnap of a child.

## THE GRIFTERS

One of the seminal neo-*noirs*, Stephen Frears's movie *The Grifters* (1990), scr Donald E. Westlake, paints a sorry picture of three hopeless people. (See page 59.)

## A SWELL-LOOKING BABE

Filmed in 1996 as *Hit Me*, dir Steven Shainberg, scr Denis Johnson. Hotel bellhop Elias Koteas is seduced by guest Laure Marsac and believes this is love. Bruce Ramsay ropes him into a plan to rob the hotel safe, and Koteas sees this as a way to escape to Paris with Marsac.

## THIS WORLD, THEN THE FIREWORKS

Dir Michael Oblowitz, scr Larry Gross, *This World, Then the Fireworks* (1997) sees brother and sister Billy Zane and Gina Gershon as incestuous conman and hooker, both scarred in early childhood by witnessing the gory murder of their father and his mistress. When Zane is seduced by sexy, masochistic cop Sheryl Lee, he sees a chance to improve the family fortunes.

# A LIBRARY OF FANTASY *NOIR*

The boundaries between genres are always fuzzy, with much overlapping. Conceptually and in terms of affect, *noir* has much in common with certain kinds of fantasy, so it's surprising there have been relatively few movies that blend the two. Even so, the rate of movie production *per annum* being what it is, that small percentage represents quite a number. A few are described in the ensuing pages.

### CAT PEOPLE
dir Jacques Tourneur, 1942

Val Lewton produced for RKO in the 1940s a group of purportedly horror movies that straddled the borders of *noir* and dark fantasy; of them, this is rightly the best-known. Simone Simon marries Kent Smith but refuses to consummate the marriage lest the sexual arousal transform her into a panther, as she claims to come from a lineage of cat people. He thinks she's being fanciful.

Lesser quasi-sequels were *Curse of the Cat People* (1944) and *Cat Girl* (1957). The unnecessary remake, *Cat People* (1982), dir Paul Schrader, is of interest to those who like watching gore and Nastassja Kinski taking her clothes off.

### KISS ME DEADLY
dir Robert Aldrich, 1955

Bearing a resemblance to the 1952 Mickey Spillane novel of the same name, this has Ralph Meeker as Mike Hammer picking up a hitchhiking escapee from a lunatic asylum, Cloris Leachman. She talks of a secret she knows, but then is killed. After much skull-duggery and betrayal, Hammer corners *femme fatale* Gaby Rogers

and the valuable "secret" – a box of radioactive material. The only
Mike Hammer movie of much interest.

### ALPHAVILLE
(vt *Alphaville: Une Étrange Aventure de Lemmy Caution*,
vt *Alphaville: A Strange Adventure of Lemmy Caution*)
dir Jean-Luc Godard, 1965, France/Italy

Godard takes Peter Cheyney's P.I. Lemmy Caution (Eddie
Constantine), hero of a successful series of straightforward
French hardboiled movies, and puts him into a surrealist, quasi-
sciencefictional setting. Alphaville is statedly a distant planet, yet
Caution travels to it by car. There a machine governs all, including
people's emotions; Caution is fazed that beautiful guide Anna
Karina is inhumanly dispassionate, despite his best attempts to
make her just another swooning Lemmy Caution dame. The plot
is a maguffin, the narrative disjointed by constant jumpcutting and
deliberate fragmentation, and the voiceover is perhaps the most
gutturally hardboiled in all *noir*.

### BLADE RUNNER
dir Ridley Scott

Based on Philip K. Dick's 1968 novel *Do Androids Dream of Electric
Sheep?*, a *noir* set in the near future, where overcrowding is
rampant. LA blade runner (essentially, P.I.) Harrison Ford must
track down a group of supersophisticated androids who've
escaped and can live undetected among "real" human beings. He
falls in love with one, a sort of passive *femme fatale* played by Sean
Young in the style of classic *noir*, and through interaction with her
and others – notably including Rutger Hauer – realizes the policy
of enslaving androids and exterminating escapees is just racism in
futuristic guise.

### THE DEAD CAN'T LIE
(vt *Gotham*)
dir Lloyd Fonvielle, 1988

A supernatural *noir* whose *femme fatale* is no less lethal because
she's dead. Seedy P.I. Tommy Lee Jones is hired by Colin Bruce to
shake off the ghost of Bruce's wife, Virginia Madsen, who was
buried at her request naked save for her jewellery – which later

Bruce dug up and purloined. Investigating, Jones meets Madsen and soon is bedded by her, a repeated act that convinces him she's alive. She's not.

### WHO FRAMED ROGER RABBIT
dir Robert Zemeckis, 1988

P.I. Bob Hoskins inhabits a world where toons – the characters of animated movies – have as much reality as human beings. He loathes toons because one of them killed his partner (shades of *The Maltese Falcon*; see page 44). Called in reluctantly on a marital case involving star toon Roger Rabbit, whose *femme fatale*-type wife Jessica (voiced by and modelled on Kathleen Turner) is seemingly unfaithful, he is soon embroiled in a murder mystery and a horrific conspiracy masterminded by Christopher Lloyd.

### DEAD AGAIN
dir Kenneth Branagh, 1991

LA P.I. Kenneth Branagh assists Emma Thompson, who has no proper memory of who she is but experiences recurring visions of forty years earlier when, in an earlier life, Branagh, then a composer, may or may not have murdered his pianist wife, Thompson. An enjoyable romantic paranormal *noir* with a Hitchcockian ending.

### FALLEN
dir Gregory Hoblit, 1998

An almost selfconsciously *noir* marriage of *noir* to the supernatural chiller, complete with copious voiceover (a technique the movie subverts in its final moments), high-angle camera shots, compositional framing, and plenty of jazz on the soundtrack. Clean cop Denzel Washington is victimized by the fallen angel Azazel, who travels from body to body by touch as he continues a killing spree in Philadelphia.

### FEMME FATALE
dir Brian De Palma, 2002

An astonishing exploration of the persona of the title, complete with full erotic charge. Con artist Rebecca Romijn-Stamos escapes Paris after her latest doublecross, finding a new life as a politician's wife in the US. But her husband is posted to Paris, and she must follow; despite her attempts at reclusiveness, knowing the crooks she doublecrossed have long memories, she is snapped by seedy freelance *paparazzo* Antonia Banderas. As the vicious hoods swarm, she draws him into a byzantinely complicated web of deceit and sexual manipulation. Even so, all seems lost when she plunges to her death in the Seine . . . only for the true, fantasticated nature to be revealed of all that has gone before.

### THE I INSIDE
dir Roland Suso Richter, 2003

Ryan Phillippe (credited as Phillipe) awakens in a hospital . . . twice, once in 2000 and once in 2002, with no knowledge of what the intervening years held. As his awareness flips repeatedly between one timeline and the other, he discovers who he is and that wife Piper Perabo (in a splendid performance), who currently inexplicably loathes him, was in the earlier time a gold-digging *femme fatale* nurse who blackmailed him into marriage. But there are two *femmes fatales* in the movie, the other being Sara Polley, whom we encounter in flashback and who was fiancée to Phillippe's brother even while sleeping with Phillippe, and who may have been a party to the brother's murder.

### THE FORGOTTEN
dir Joseph Ruben, 2004

The grief of bereaved mother Julianne Moore is enhanced because no one else can remember the son she lost in a plane crash; photos disappear or no longer show him, and psychiatrist Gary Sinise is giving her therapy to disabuse her of her "paranoid delusion". By chance she meets ex-sports star Anthony Edwards, whom she recognizes as the father of a girl her son played with who was likewise killed in the crash. He finally remembers the daughter he lost. Chased by trigger-happy spurious government agents, the two – with the help of initially sceptical cop Alfre Woodard – uncover a conspiracy that stretches well beyond our mundane reality.

# PATRICIA HIGHSMITH AND THE MOVIES

Born in Texas in 1921 and raised in New York City, Mary Patricia Plangman Highsmith emigrated to Europe in 1963, thereafter spending much of her time in France and Switzerland. Her first novel, *Strangers on a Train* (1950), had the good fortune to be filmed by Alfred Hitchcock with a script cowritten by Raymond Chandler. This was the start of an involvement with the movies that would last the remainder of her life. Her best-known series of novels featured the psychopath Tom Ripley, who murdered his way through *The Talented Mr. Ripley* (1955), *Ripley Under Ground* (1970), *Ripley's Game* (1974), *The Boy Who Followed Ripley* (1980) and *Ripley Under Water* (1991). Other novels are *The Blunderer* (1954), *Deep Water* (1957), *This Sweet Sickness* (1960), *The Cry of the Owl* (1962), *The Glass Cell* (1964), *The Two Faces of January* (1964), *The Story-Teller* (1965; vt *A Suspension of Mercy*), *The Tremor of Forgery* (1969), *A Dog's Ransom* (1972) and *Edith's Diary* (1977). She died of leukemia in Locarno, Switzerland, in 1995.

## STRANGERS ON A TRAIN

A classic crime movie, the 1951 adaptation was dir Alfred Hitchcock and starred Farley Granger and Robert Walker as Guy and Bruno, the two men who meet on a train and agree at Bruno's instigation each to murder a close relative of the other – Guy's wife and Bruno's father.

A bad remake came in 1969, retitled *Once You Kiss a Stranger* and with Highsmith uncredited. Robert Sparr directed Carol Lynley as a *femme fatale* who entices Paul Burke into a criss-cross murder plot.

In 1996 came the TV-movie remake *Once You Meet a Stranger,* cowritten by director Tommy Lee Wallace with Whitfield Cook. Jacqueline Bissett as Sheila is lured by an excellently cast Theresa Russell as Margo into the scheme. Aside from the gender changes, the adaptation is relatively faithful.

A further remake, reverting to the title *Strangers on a Train*, has been announced for 2006 with director Noam Murro and scripter David Seltzer.

Also of relevance is the black comedy *Throw Momma from the Train* (1987), dir Danny DeVito and scr Stu Silver. Creative-writing tutor Bill Crystal suggests student DeVito should watch the Hitchcock *Strangers on a Train*, and DeVito assumes this means Crystal wants him to murder Crystal's wife in return for Crystal murdering DeVito's termagant mother.

### RIPLEY

The first screen adaptation of *The Talented Mr. Ripley* was done by Highsmith herself for the US TV series *Studio One*. It was broadcast in 1956, dir Franklin J. Schaffner, and starred Keefe Brasselle.

The 1960 French/Italian movie *Plein Soleil* (vt *Purple Noon*, vt *Blazing Sun*), coscripted by director René Clément and Paul Gégauff, was the next Ripley adaptation, again of *The Talented Mr. Ripley*; Alain Delon was Ripley. This was Delon's third movie, and its huge success gave him the breakthrough to international stardom.

Wim Wenders's 1977 West German/French movie *Der Amerikanische Freund* (vt *The American Friend*) came next, based on *Ripley's Game*. Dennis Hopper as Ripley lures Bruno Gantz into a murderous scheme.

1999 saw a major release for *The Talented Mr. Ripley*, dir Anthony Minghella (who also scripted), with Matt Damon as Ripley, Jude Law as his first victim, and Gwyneth Paltrow as Law's girlfriend, a secondary motive for this murder.

The Italian/UK/US coproduction *Il Gioco di Ripley* (2002; vt *Ripley's Game*), dir Liliana Cavani (who also scripted), was next. It saw John Malkovich as an excellently chilling Ripley in a production that avoided the *faux* sentimentalism of the 1999 movie. This may well be the best Ripley movie of all; in typically crass fashion, while the movie received full theatrical release elsewhere, in the US, aside from a brief arthouse mini-release, it went straight to DVD.

Also troubled in its release was *Ripley Under Ground* (2005; vt *White on White*, vt *Mr. Ripley Returns*, vt *Mr. Ripley's Art*), dir Roger Spottiswoode, scr William Blake Herron and Donald E. Westlake. This treatment is almost more a black comedy than a thriller. Barry Pepper is Ripley, here pretending a murdered artist is still alive in order to cash in. At the time of writing the movie was in constantly-delayed-release hell, and may go straight to DVD.

### OTHERS

*The Blunderer* was adapted in 1963 by director Claude Autant-Lara as *Le Meurtrier* (1963; vt *Enough Rope*), a French/West German/Italian coproduction scr Jean Aurenche and Pierre Bost. It starred Maurice Ronet, Marina Vlady and Robert Hossein.

*This Sweet Sickness* was adapted in 1977 as *Dites-lui que je t'Aime* (vt *This Sweet Sickness*) by director Claude Miller, who coscripted with Luc Béraud. Gérard Depardieu stars as an accountant who lives in a fantasy world in which his parents haven't died and he will marry the woman over whom he obsesses even though she's already happily married with a child . . .

The West German/Portuguese movie *Die gläserne Zelle* (1978), dir Hans W. Geissendörfer, who coscripted with Klaus Bädekerl, is based on *The Glass Cell*. Helmut Griem stars as an unjustly imprisoned man who on release becomes consumed with jealousy over what wife Brigitte Fossey might have got up to during his incarceration. Six years later Geissendörfer directed and scripted *Ediths Tagebuch* (1984; vt *Edith's Diary*), based on *Edith's Diary*.

*Deep Water* was adapted in 1981 as *Eaux Profondes* (vt *Deep Water*), dir Michel Deville, who coscripted with Florence Delay. Isabelle Huppert and Jean-Louis Trintignant star in a tale of a husband who will tolerate his wife's infidelities only so long.

Highsmith movies are clearly popular in Germany. *The Two Faces of January* was filmed as *Die Zwei Gesichter des Januar* (1986; vt *The Two Faces of January*), dir Wolfgang Storch (who coscripted with Karl-Heinz Willschrei) and Gabriela Zerhau. In the following year appeared the TV movie *Der Schrei der Eule*, dir Tom Toelle, scr Peter Märtesheimer and Pea Fröhlich, the first of two movies made in 1987 based on *The Cry of the Owl*. The other was a French/Italian production, *Le Cri du Hibou* (vt *The Cry of the Owl*), dir Claude Chabrol (who also coscripted with Odile Barski). This was not one of Chabrol's major outings. Again from Germany came *Der Geschichtenerzähler* (1989; vt *The Story Teller*), dir Rainer Boldt, who coscripted with Dorothea Neukirchen, Hans Kwiet and Wolf Christian Schröder.

*The Day of Reckoning* was made into a UK/French TV movie of that name (vt *Le Jour du Châtiment*) by director Samuel Fuller, who coscripted with Christa Lang. *The Tremor of Forgery* was made into the German movie *Trip nach Tunis* (1993), dir Peter Goedel, who coscripted with Harald Goeckeritz. David Hunt plays an archaeologist who discovers much strangeness at a dig in North Africa. And *La Rançon du Chien* (1996), based on *A Dog's Ransom*, was a French TV movie dir Peter Kassovitz and scr Jean-François Goyet.

# THE EDGAR AWARDS

The Edgars (more formally, the Edgar Allan Poe Awards) have been presented in various categories by the Mystery Writers of America since 1946; from the first, Best Motion Picture was one of the categories. The individuals recognized in this movie award have varied over time – sometimes the screenwriter(s), sometimes also the author of the original book. Here the directors are indicated in parentheses.

**1946** *Murder, My Sweet* (vt *Farewell, My Lovely*), John Paxton (dir Edward Dmytryk)

**1947** *The Killers*, Anthony Veiller (dir Robert Siodmak)

**1948** *Crossfire*, John Paxton (dir Edward Dmytryk)

**1949** *Call Northside 777*, Jerome Cady, Jay Dratler, (dir Henry Hathaway), Leonard Hoffman, Otto Lang, Quentin Reynolds

**1950** *The Window*, Mel Dinelli, Cornell Woolrich (dir Ted Tetzlaff)

**1951** *The Asphalt Jungle*, Ben Maddow (dir John Huston)

**1952** *Detective Story*, Sidney Kingsley, Robert Wyler, Philip Yordan (dir William Wyler)

**1953** *5 Fingers*, Otto Lang, Michael G. Wilson (dir Joseph L. Mankiewicz)

**1954** *The Big Heat*, Sidney Boehm, William P. McGivern (dir Fritz Lang)

**1955** *Rear Window*, John Michael Hayes (dir Alfred Hitchcock)

**1956** *The Desperate Hours*, Joseph Hayes (dir William Wyler)

**1958** *Twelve Angry Men*, Reginald Rose (dir Sidney Lumet)

**1959** *The Defiant Ones*, Nathan E. Douglas, Harold Jacob Smith (dir Stanley Kramer)

**1960** *North by Northwest*, Ernest Lehman (dir Alfred Hitchcock)

**1961** *Psycho*, Robert Bloch, Joseph Stefano (dir Alfred Hitchcock)

**1962** *The Innocents*, William Archibald, Truman Capote (dir Jack Clayton)

**1964** *Charade*, Peter Stone (dir Stanley Donen)

**1965** *Hush ... Hush, Sweet Charlotte*, Henry Farrell, Lukas Heller (dir Robert Aldrich)

**1966** *The Spy Who Came in from the Cold*, Paul Dehn, Guy Trosper (dir Martin Ritt)

**1967** *Harper* (vt *The Moving Target*), William Goldman (dir Jack Smight)

**1968** *In the Heat of the Night*, Stirling Silliphant (dir Norman Jewison)

**1969** *Bullitt*, Robert L. Fish, Harry Kleiner, Alan R. Trustman (dir Peter Yates)

**1970** *Z*, Costa-Gavras (dir), Jorge Semprun

**1971** *Indagine su un Cittadino al di Sopra di Ogno Sospetto* (vt *Investigation of a Citizen Above Suspicion*), Ellio Petri (dir), Ugo Pirro

**1972** *The French Connection*, Ernest Tidyman (dir William Friedkin)

**1973** *Sleuth*, Anthony Shaffer (dir Joseph L. Mankiewicz)

**1974** *The Last of Sheila*, Anthony Perkins, Stephen Sondheim (dir Herbert Ross)

**1975** *Chinatown*, Robert Towne (dir Roman Polanski)

**1976** *Three Days of the Condor*, David Rayfiel, Lorenzo Semple Jr. (dir Sydney Pollack)

**1977** *Family Plot*, Ernest Lehman (dir Alfred Hitchcock)

**1978** *The Late Show*, Robert Benton (dir Robert Benton)

**1979** *Magic*, William Goldman (dir Richard Attenborough)

**1980** *The Great Train Robbery* (vt *The First Great Train Robbery*), Michael Crichton (dir)

**1981** *The Black Marble*, Joseph Wambaugh (dir Harold Becker)

**1982** *Cutter's Way* (vt *Cutter and Bone*), Jeffrey Alan Fiskin (dir Ivan Passer)

**1983** *The Long Good Friday*, Barrie Keefe (dir John MacKenzie)

**1984** *Gorky Park*, Dennis Potter (dir Michael Apted)

**1985** *A Soldier's Story*, Charles Fuller (dir Norman Jewison)

**1986** *Witness*, William Kelley, Earl W. Wallace (dir Peter Weir)

**1987** *Something Wild*, E. Max Frye (dir Jonathan Demme)

**1988** *Stakeout*, Jim Kouf (dir John Badham)

**1989** *The Thin Blue Line*, Errol Morris (dir)

**1990** *Heathers*, Daniel Waters (dir Michael Lehmann)

**1991** *The Grifters*, Donald E. Westlake (dir Stephen Frears)

**1992** *The Silence of the Lambs*, Ted Tally (dir Jonathan Demme)

**1993** *The Player*, Michael Tolkin (dir Robert Altman)

**1994** *Falling Down*, Ebbe Rose Smith (dir Joel Schumacher)

**1995** *Pulp Fiction*, Quentin Tarantino (dir)

**1996** *The Usual Suspects*, Christopher McQuarrie (dir Bryan Singer)

**1997** *Sling Blade*, Billy Bob Thorton (dir)

**1998** *L.A. Confidential*, Curtis Hanson (dir), Brian Helgeland

**1999** *Out of Sight*, Scott Frank (dir Steven Soderbergh)

**2000** *Lock, Stock and Two Smoking Barrels*, Guy Ritchie (dir)

**2001** *Traffic*, Stephen Gaghan (dir Steven Soderbergh)

**2002** *Memento*, Christopher Nolan (dir)

**2003** *Chicago*, Bill Condon (dir Rob Marshall)

**2004** *Dirty Pretty Things*, Steve Knight (dir Stephen Frears)

**2005** *Un Long Dimanche de Fiançailles* (vt *A Very Long Engagement*), Jean-Pierre Jeunet (dir)

*In a few (non-consecutive) years a separate presentation was made for Best Foreign Film. The winners in this category were:*

**1949** *Quai des Orfèvres*, Henri-Georges Clouzot (dir), Jean Ferry

**1956** *Les Diaboliques* (vt *Diabolique*, vt *The Fiends*), Henri-Georges Clouzot

**1959** *Maigret Tend un Piège* (vt *Maigret Lays a Trap*, vt *Maigret Sets a Trap*), Georges Simenon (dir Jean Delannoy)

**1960** *Sapphire*, Janet Green (dir Basil Dearden)

**1962** *Plein Soleil* (vt *Purple Noon*, vt *Blazing Sun*), René Clement (dir), Paul Degauff

**1964** *Mélodie en Sous-Sol* (vt *Any Number Can Win*, vt *Anyone Can Win*, vt *Big Grab*, vt *The Big Snatch*), Michael Audiard, Albert Simonin, Henri Verneuil (dir)

**1965** *Seance on a Wet Afternoon*, Bryan Forbes (dir)

**1966** *The Ipcress File*, Bill Canaway, James Doran (dir Sidney J. Furie)

# BIBLIOGRAPHY

Barbour, Alan G.: *Humphrey Bogart*, New York, Galahad, 1973

Buss, Robin: *French Film Noir*, London, Marion Boyars, 2001

DeAndrea, William L.: *Encyclopedia Mysteriosa: A Comprehensive Guide to the Art of Detection in Print, Film, Radio and Television*, New York, Prentice-Hall, 1994

French, Karl, and French, Philip: *Cult Movies*, New York, Billboard, 2000

Hardy, Phil (ed): *The BFI Companion to Crime*, Berkeley, University of California Press, 1997

Haskell, Molly: *From Reverence to Rape: The Treatment of Women in the Movies*, Chicago, University of Chicago Press, 1987

Hirsch, Foster: *Detours and Lost Highways: A Map of Neo-Noir*, New York, Limelight, 1999

Layman, Richard (ed): *Discovering The Maltese Falcon and Sam Spade*, San Francisco, Vince Emery, 2005

Lyons, Arthur: *Death on the Cheap: The Lost B Movies of Film Noir*, New York, Da Capo, 2000

McCarthy, Todd, and Flynn, Charles (eds): *Kings of the Bs: Working Within the System: An Anthology of Film History and Criticism*, New York, Dutton, 1975

McClelland, Doug: *The Golden Age of "B" Movies*, New York, Bonanza, 1981

Muller, Eddie: *Dark City: The Lost World of Film Noir*, New York, St Martin's, 1998

Phillips, Gene D.: *Creatures of Darkness: Raymond Chandler, Detective Fiction, and Film Noir*, Lexington, University Press of Kentucky, 2000

Robinson, David: *The History of World Cinema*, New York, Stein & Day, 1973

Silver, Alain: *Film Noir: An Encyclopedic Reference to the American Style* (3rd edn), New York, Overlook, 1992

Also of considerable usefulness are The Internet Movie Data Base (www.imdb.com) and the New York Times's online movie reviews archive (www.nytimes.com/ref/movies/reviews/index.html).

> *"Do I laugh now
> or wait 'til it gets funny?"*
> Double Indemnity (1944)